the Answer

IT'S ALL IN YOUR HEAD

Now you know.
Kindly,

DR. C

The Answer
It's All In Your Head
Now you know. Kindly, Dr. C

by Dr. C (Jorge Cardenas)

Copyright © 2017
Jorge Cardenas

All rights reserved. This book may not be copied or reprinted for commercial purposes or financial gain. The use of quotations or page copying for personal or group study is permitted and encouraged.

Unless otherwise identified, Scripture quotations are from the New International Version of the Bible. All emphasis within Scripture are the author's own.

ISBN-13: 978-0-9992740-0-2 (hc)
ISBN-13: 978-0-9992740-1-9 (ebk)

Cover art, "My Ascension", painted by Jennifer L. Simmons © April 2015
Interior Photos © Jennifer L. Simmons
Flow charts © Jorge Cardenas
Cover and book layout by Suzanne Fyhrie Parrott

DEDICATION

When I was in my youth and filling my brain with knowledge, I was also filled with a great deal of pride. My pride was not a false pride. It came from my accomplishments. The pride resulted because that is exactly what this world offers. It felt good for a while; especially, making me feel like I was in competition with the rest of the world and I was winning.

With the discovery of the creative force, I began to apply it to different parts of my life. I began to see the world in a very different way. The awareness of my ability to create and control my reality made me realize that any previous successes were almost like accidents designed to happen by a Creator whom I had not met.

One big difference between people who are successful and those who are less successful is the presence of a mentor, generally the parents, who by accident teach the more successful child more positive thinking than the average person. This awareness made me realize that I was given wonderful parents who continue to influence me to be better and better. Therefore, it is to my parents I owe my success and to them I give thanks. I began to see my pride lessen and my wisdom grow.

Through this realization, I began to see how influential other people in my life were. My wife, my children, my Ava, my teachers, my siblings, and my coworkers. I began to realize that all along I have been surrounded by the most amazing people and that all my accomplishments were really not the result of my own personal effort, but rather a team effort that had as its purpose to give me the most amazing life.

Knowing the Creative Force caused me to ask the question, "Who created this most amazing life for me?" The answer is rather simple: my Creator. He goes by many names, but I choose to call Him Abba. My pride disappeared when I realized that for a long time my Abba had been creating and putting together the most incredible journey for my life.

It is to God, my Abba, my Creator, Christ, to whom I dedicate this book. It is to Him who I give all credit and all glory forever and ever, amen.

Contents

CHAPTER ONE
THE WORK THAT MUST BE DONE 10

CHAPTER TWO
ALL THINGS BEGIN AS A THOUGHT 14

CHAPTER THREE
THE PATTERNS THAT I SEE 17

CHAPTER FOUR
THE ENERGY OF A THOUGHT 20

CHAPTER FIVE
MORE DETAILS ABOUT THE CREATIVE FORCE 24

CHAPTER SIX
THE MOST PROFOUND OBSERVATIONS 30

CHAPTER SEVEN
REALITY 34

CHAPTER EIGHT
THE CARDENAS LAW 38

CHAPTER NINE
YOUR PERSONAL REALITY 44

CHAPTER TEN
THE DISCOVERY OF TIME AND THE APPLICATION OF SIZE . . 48

CHAPTER ELEVEN
MY DISAPPOINTMENT 52

CHAPTER TWELVE
A FEW BIBLE VERSES 57

CHAPTER THIRTEEN
   A CREATOR 62

CHAPTER FOURTEEN
   WHAT DOES THE BIBLE TELL ME 66

CHAPTER FIFTEEN
   SINNER VERSUS SAINT 70

CHAPTER SIXTEEN
   THE GODS WE MAKE AND THE GOD OF THE BIBLE 75

CHAPTER SEVENTEEN
   A BAD EXAMPLE 81

CHAPTER EIGHTEEN
   ANGER, GUILT, AND DEALING WITH MY PAST 85

CHAPTER NINETEEN
   FEAR, THE WILL OF GOD, CREATING MY FUTURE 92

CHAPTER TWENTY
   PRAYER AND THE CREATIVE FORCE .98

CHAPTER TWENTY ONE
   REARING CHILDREN AND THE CREATIVE FORCE. 103

CHAPTER TWENTY TWO
   RACISM. 108

CHAPTER TWENTY THREE
   THOUGHTS TO AVOID AND THOUGHTS TO REPEAT. 114

CHAPTER TWENTY FOUR
   CONCLUSION 118

PROLOGUE

When one chooses to sit down and observe life, one's life and the lives of others, we see the sum of random events, actions, consequences, and practices. The unique experiences of each individual appear to be the consequence of events almost to the point that we feel out of control. We are unable to explain such events in a logical way. Why is it that some people become successful while others with the same degrees of education and levels of intelligence seem less fortunate?

We begin our explanations with the addition of factors like genetics, luck, karma, and God. We do not seem to come up with a cohesive explanation. Therefore, we add factors like grace and the existence of a God who appears distant, difficult to reach, and either unable or incapable of changing our circumstances.

At the end, we settle on a mediocre life, unfulfilled, and with a great deal of defeat and fear under our belt when we accept that "it is what it is" or that it's "the way life works." Does it have to be so? Can one change one's life? If one can change one's life, can one control it in a way that one can be certain that one will like the outcome or the reality that one creates?

The answers is,

yes.

I am going to walk you through the steps required for you to change your life in a manner so that you will like what you have created and in the process you will learn that life is rather simple. The only problem at this point is that you have not been trained properly. Once you accept this training and begin to apply it, you will develop a sense of control like you have never felt before; and you, of your own desire, will continue to seek higher and higher wisdom that will eventually lead you to the Creator of it all.

INTRODUCTION

My story, like the story of any person, can be told by the description of the events surrounding me, but it is not the real story. It is simply the recollection of events that others see. Yet, the true story is unfolding in the mind of the individual where there appears to be a war that is fought in the mind. That is the real story, but it can only be described, yet not shared by others because the others simply cannot feel the collection of events unfolding in my mind.

My story for this book began 15 years ago. I had been divorced for a few years. I was obese. I was failing in my ability to guide my children. I was a physician and I was financially stable. I was reared as a Christian and I prayed with frequency. Yet, inside my brain I felt lonely, fearful, frustrated, insecure, and pessimistic about my future and the future of my children. My money had lost its meaning because it had failed to bring what I was looking for the most, mental peace.

I was looking for satisfaction in life, the purpose of my actions, and the contentment of my surroundings. Yet, everything felt foreign, unfamiliar, like an out of body experience where you are perfectly aware of the surroundings, yet you feel so out of place that nothing fits. The human pleasures became unsatisfactory; possessions became stumbling blocks; and power and control became distasteful.

I have always had the feeling that there were things near me that I was missing or not seeing: a sense that happiness, purpose, and satisfaction were possible. This only added to the frustration I felt. I remember as a child in Colombia asking my school friends to join me to study the things of God, such as reading the Bible, only to be dismissed due to the lack of interest. Growing up in Colombia, as a traditional Catholic, Bible reading was not typical, or I should say, Bible reading was not practiced in my home. Yet, this interest in the secrets of life has been with me since early childhood.

I came across multiple books such as, "The Secret", "The Gift", "The Master Key System", to name a few. What I concluded from my sporadic reading through the years was that thoughts seem to possess an energy. I remember reading about a Japanese scientist studying the structure of water. This scientist, on a bad day in his life when his temper was not at its best, found the structure to be an irregular crystal, a poor image. During another day when the scientist's mood was better, the same experiment showed that the structure of the crystal formed was more beautiful, like the perfect snowflake. The only difference seemed to be the scientist's mood, or so he thought.

As a trained biologist and chemist, and later physician, the interpretation of all of these bits and pieces of information did not follow the logical processes that I had learned during my training. In addition, other bits of information kept on crawling into my brain adding to the almost confused state of my mind. I had heard of the power of positive thinking. I had also heard about how happiness led to longer, healthier lives.

Little by little, the information was coming together in my brain like the pieces to a puzzle. My scientific brain began to ponder that thoughts seem to be a form of energy that we have not begun to study or understand.

My scientific mind started to take over and began to process the information read, and to ponder how it all came together. At about this time, my biggest problem was my obesity. I was almost 240 lbs, miserable, and uncomfortable when moving; fearful of diabetes and death; and full of knowledge in biology, chemistry, anatomy, diabetes, metabolism, and exercise. My knowledge was worthless to correct my problem. The dilemma was quite real. I knew what to do, yet I was incapable of doing anything about it; almost as if I were paralyzed to move in the correct direction that I could easily see in my brain. Just as a drowning person who knows how to swim, yet is unable to move. My obesity was getting worse. I was the fat doctor having to tell his patients to lose weight. I felt desperate.

My brain would not let go of this idea that thoughts had energy. Therefore, I chose to set up an experiment and observe the consequences. Just like any committed scientist, I decided to be the subject. Being cheap, I saw this as a bonus because I did not have to pay myself. It was an open experiment to see what would happen without expectations, simply observation.

The thought I chose was, "I look great". I started to repeat this day in and day out and began to observe what changes occurred without expectations. In my brain, I began to see images of what I considered great looking. I was paying attention to the physical aspects of male models and I began to choose what aspects of the looks were appealing and what parts were not. An image began to form in my brain and every time I said, "I look great", I would see this image.

At about the same time, I decided to eliminate starches and sugars, much like the Adkins diet, except with quite a bit of fruit that I had become accustomed to consuming. I did not change the amount of food consumed, just the type of food. In the first month, I lost 30 pounds, almost without effort or sacrifice.

I still remember looking in the mirror when I saw I had clavicles. The smile that came upon my face was neat because my brain, almost like a reflex, repeated "I look great".

The epiphany: the thought, "I look great" was becoming my reality.

Therefore, this book is about the energy that thoughts have and how to control it. This book is really in 2 parts. Part one is the basic teaching about thought or knowledge about thought, and the second part is the practice required based on what you are being taught. If you limit yourself to reading this book without doing the exercises, you have acquired only knowledge and therefore, you will continue to be incapable of changing your life in any meaningful way because knowledge alone is worthless to change your behavior.

If you commit yourself to practicing what I teach, you will develop the power to change everything that you do not like in your life and also the ability to obtain more of what brings pleasure to your life.

CHAPTER ONE

THE WORK THAT MUST BE DONE

If a book is not able to enhance or improve your life, it should not be read. So, it is with this book. It is in the application of what is being taught that brings about the change you desire. I know that up to this point I have not provided you with much insight, but I am going to ask you to trust me, TEMPORARILY until you begin to see change at which time you will know to believe all the time.

The first task at hand is very simple: we, you and I, must create an environment where the energy of your thoughts is created and multiplied in a specific direction of our choosing. I recommend two activities.

First activity: take several 3x5 inch cards and write on each one the following thought: "Thank you God, my life gets better and better all the time".

figure 1

I suggest that you use a marker thick and bright enough that each letter is easy to read when you are passing by. Then place these cards in the places where you spend some time. I have placed mine on my bathroom mirror, the refrigerator, on the wall in front of my desk, and on my desk. Every situation is going to be different, but the goal is the same, repetition. The idea is that when you pass by your brain will see the sign and automatically repeat the thought, "Thank you God, my life gets better and better all the time".

The second activity is more intentional and less automatic. I suspect it is more powerful, but at the end these two activities will join to create a specific life that I think most people want. You are to get a lined notebook like the one used in school. I recommend a wire bound 10 1/2 in. x 8 in. notebook. They usually have 25 lines on which to write. You are going to write and rewrite a specific thought:

"Thank you God, today I am wiser, kinder, meeker, stronger, healthier, wealthier, and fearless."

This is a long thought and most likely will take two lines to write in the notebook I suggested. The idea is repetition. In the morning, I recommend you complete one side of the page, line by line, repeating the same thought. It would be much like having a quiet time or prayer time except that the prayer becomes exclusive for your mind to stay focused.

In the evening, complete the opposite side of the page. Therefore, in a 24 hour period you should have completed both sides of one page. I have included one picture (figure 2, page 12) as an example. Do not be distracted if your notebook looks differently. The idea is the repetition of this specific thought.

These two activities are not the only times you can repeat these thoughts. Indeed, I recommend that these thoughts become part of your DNA and you will repeat them constantly, day in and day out.

The first thing you are going to notice in your brain is the existence of some thoughts that contradict these written and prescribed thoughts. The idea is that when a negative thought appears in your head, you then have the correct thought and all you have to do is to take the intentional decision to repeat the thoughts I have given you. I want to make you aware that you do not have to like these thoughts and you do not have to believe these thoughts. For now, all I want you to do is to repeat these thoughts. Later on, as you develop expertise, you will be able to change them in such way as to achieve your goals and desires.

figure 2

During my experimentation with thoughts, I added another form of repetition, but I do not think that it is required for you to do unless you are knowledgeable of technology. I simply recorded the written notebook exercise and created a MP3 file and downloaded it to the music in my phone. Then, I created a playlist and added this file only. When I am by myself, I play this file. It is my voice and because it is in a loop, it replays and replays until I get tired of hearing my own voice. It is repetition, nonetheless.

To start, I only recommend the first two exercises and later on you can add your MP3 exercise. What I expect to happen is that your brain will become more organized and you will begin to prioritize actions.

You will also feel the motivation to follow through with these actions. These actions will have consequences, but the consequences will create an improved situation in your life that is better than when you began to read this book. I cannot tell you what to do because each one of us has a different path to follow. Therefore, your steps will be different from mine.

CHAPTER TWO

ALL THINGS BEGIN AS A THOUGHT

I want you to look around the room where you are and focus on a specific object. Such as a table, or more specifically, a coffee table. If you think about how this table came about, one could run its history easily by moving back in time. Before the table became what we call a table, the carpenter had to paint it. Before painting it, he had to glue the pieces together. Before he was able to glue the pieces together, he had to cut out the right shapes and lengths. I want to point out that the shapes, sizes, and connections made were not random. These actions or steps were very specific.

Before the carpenter was able to buy and cut the wood, glue and paint the wood, he had convinced himself that he was going to be able to make the said table. That table, again, was not a random table. The image of this specific table appeared in the carpenter's mind. Before Mr. Carpenter made up his mind, he had to choose specifically what kind of table he was going to make. He had to choose from pool tables, dining room tables, surgery tables, lamp tables, or coffee tables. The selection process also included the material to be used. The carpenter could have used glass, metal, plastic, or wood. Since our table is wood, one can assume that the carpenter decided to make a wooden coffee table. He was able to see the finished product in his head even before buying the wood and all the other materials. The coffee table began as a thought in the mind of the carpenter. Allow me to add, that in this case, the thought was the image of the table.

Another observation I want to make you aware of is that time passed between the initial thought, "I am going to make a coffee table" and the moment the table became a physical reality. The process of creating the table is not magic where the carpenter wiggled his nose and the table appeared. Mr. Carpenter had to persist in his idea. Another way to put it would be that Mr. Carpenter repeated the thought and he did not change his thought. Lastly, Mr. Carpenter and no one else took the steps that created the table.

If this table began as a thought, one can extend the same analysis to all the things that you see in the room and begin to explain the existence of the couch, the pillows, the rug, and the paintings. For example, when looking at the couch if someone were to ask you, "How did the couch begin?" You can easily and comfortably answer, "With a thought".

As the second example for this chapter, I am going to use myself. I am a physician and I practice Obstetrics / Gynecology. The same analysis can be done as with the previous example of the table. All we would have to do is to move back in time to find the beginning of the fact that I am a physician.

Before I was able to work as a physician and before I could be hired as a physician, I had to get a license from the state board of medicine. Before the board of medicine would grant me a license, I had to prove to them that I had finished my training in Ob/Gyn. Even further back, in order to be accepted in my residency program, I had to show proof that I had completed medical school. Before applying to medical school, I had to complete my college degree, take the MCAT, and secure the letters of recommendation from my college professors.

I want you to know that the steps taken in order to become a physician were not random steps. All the steps were prescribed. I knew what to do simply because ever since I was a child, I have been repeating, "I am going to be a doctor". Going one step further back, before I was able to speak, "I am going to be a doctor"; " I am going to be a doctor" was a thought. It was an image in my head. I still remember with clarity that I was watching an episode of Marcus Welby, MD when the thought appeared.

There is really nothing special to this thought. I simply chose to repeat it. When my brothers and sisters were playing cowboys and Indians, my selected role was always the doctor. The image I saw in my brain was the one of Doctor Welby doing his hero work. In summary, I can conclude that the fact that I am a physician began as a thought.

In reference to time elapsed, I want to add that the initial thought, "I am going to be a doctor" began to be repeated when I was around 5-6 years old. Twenty five years later I began to practice as a physician.

As a sideline, try saying something, speaking any word just to play with your brain. My suspicion is that an image would appear in your brain before you would be able to say it. Therefore, it appears that the brain does not see words or letters. The brain only sees images.

The third and last example for this chapter will ask you to imagine moving into a new house that you had built. Again, if we want to know the origin of this house, all we have to do is to move the house back in time, step by step to reveal the first, initial step. Before you moved into the house, the house had to be built. Before the contractor was able to buy the materials to build it, he had a plan. The drawings most likely came from you and your dreams as to the exact style of the house you wanted. Before you drew the plans for the house, you must have purchased the land. Even before purchasing the land, the house really began as a thought when you made the decision, "I am going to build my house". An image appeared in your head and the more you repeated the thought, the more details you were adding to the picture of the house. In conclusion, the house you are about to enter began as a thought. Again, there was nothing magical about the thought, "I am going to build my house". What makes this thought unique is that you did not change your mind, you simply kept repeating it until it became your reality.

As with the previous examples, I want to point out that between the moment you had your first thought, "I am going to build my house" and the time to move into your house, some time had elapsed. Therefore, time is a variable that we will have to learn to control.

In conclusion, I hope I have convinced you that whether we are talking about a table, my career, your house, or for that matter anything else that you can see or feel, all things begin as a thought. Now that you possess this knowledge, you have the power to explain the past. If you see a pair of shoes, you can confidently explain that the shoes began as a thought. If you see a shirt, the shirt began as a thought. If you see a policeman, you can say that his career began as a thought. You are now and forever aware that thought is the unit of creation, of all creation.

CHAPTER THREE

THE PATTERNS THAT I SEE

I want to bring you back to the introduction section of this book. During that introduction, I pointed out the results of my experiments with thought. Just as a reminder, I began with a thought, "I look great". After a few times of repetition, an image had formed in my brain which became the representation of what I considered great looking. The experiment was rather simple because it only required the voice repetition of this particular thought.

As the result of the repetition, I felt the desire to stop eating starches and sugars. Please note that I had extensive knowledge of the Adkins Diet and South Beach Diet, but until that moment, I had not felt the desire to do anything about it. I remember clearly making a list of the foods I felt needed to be eliminated in my diet. I remember feeling the motivation to stop eating those types of food. I did not change the amount of food intake. Within 4 weeks, I had lost over 30 lbs. The result or the consequence of my actions was the weight loss. The outcome, if you will, was that I was becoming great looking or rather that the thought was becoming my reality.

The pattern I saw was **thought**, followed by the **repetition** of the thought, followed by the **actions** that the thought suggested, and finally the consequences of the actions or the **outcome**.

I can use the same analysis with the other examples mentioned in Chapter 2. For the example of the table, the carpenter first had to make the decision of what kind of table he was going to make. This generated a specific image in his head. The next step was the repetition of the thought. I guess another way to put it would be to say that the carpenter did not change his mind. The next step was a series of specific steps, and the final step, or the consequence of the actions, was the creation of a table. I like to point out at this time that the actual table had to look very similar to the image the carpenter had in his head when this creative process began.

For the example of my childhood thought, "I am going to be a doctor", my image was the one of Dr. Welby, MD. This was rather simple because my brain had to borrow the television image. Since this was a television series, the repetition became almost automatic. I realize that I must have mentioned it all the time to everyone because of a gift I received when I was six years of age.

There was a visiting nurse, my mother's friend, who gave me her old doctor's bag to play with. Her action only helped my brain to continue repeating the thought, "I am going to be a doctor". The next step in the creative process is the set of specific actions. These steps appeared almost like magic in my brain. Another way to say it, is that my brain saw what steps to take, or in a more mystical way, the thought revealed the steps to take in a very specific order. This is a very important point to emphasize because I was not surrounded by any medical professionals in the family. To this date, I do not recall any conversations with either of my parents suggesting what profession I should choose.

The repetition of the thought, "I am going to be a doctor" created the steps to take, but in the bigger picture, the money, situations, and people were put in place to make my steps possible. Now, I simply want to say that it occurred almost by magic. Clearly, this is not magic, but everything required to fulfill my thought appeared at the right time, in the right sequence, and at the right place.

The pattern of creation remains the same: **thought**, **repetition** of the thought, **actions** required by the thought, and finally the consequences of those actions, **outcome**, which create a reality very similar to the thought. I can conclude that the thought and the outcome it produces are identical with some minor details to be worked out by the variable called time.

I like to refer to this process as the creative process, but because we are dealing with an energy contained in each thought, the name should be the creative force. The energy generated by the repetition of thoughts is a creative force which shows the steps to take and forces you to take these steps. In the previous chapter when you became aware that all things are created by thought, it gave you the power to explain the past. Now, you know the creative process or creative force which gives you the power to predict the future. This is possible because of your awareness that the thought and the outcome are equal.

For example, if I begin to repeat, "I am going to make hamburgers tonight" and I do not change my mind, my brain will see the image of a hamburger and the repetition will cause my brain to show the steps to take in order to accomplish my goal. I will also have the motivation to pursue those steps and the consequence of those steps will be that I will make burgers tonight. Due to the fact that the thought and the outcome are equal for all circumstances, now I can use the creative force to predict the future every time I am aware of the persistent thoughts in my mind.

I must narrow the reach of the Creative Force from all thoughts become reality to that only those thoughts that you repeat become reality. Not every thought that you repeat a few times will become your reality because this process allows you to change your thought at any time. I can begin with the thought, "I want to make hamburgers tonight" and for some reason when my thought changes to, "I want pizza", a new process of creation begins.

The energy accumulated by the repetition of thoughts comes in different names. For example, if I repeat a thought like, "I am going to be a doctor" you would call this force: motivation. If I repeat a thought about being rich, you would create a force called: ambition. If I repeat a thought about sex, you would call this force: lust. If I repeat a thought about disliking someone, you would call that force: hate. If I repeat a thought that causes doubt, you would call this force: fear. Therefore, the name of the force may be different, but its origin is the same: the repetition of a thought or image in your brain.

At this point in time, I recommend that you put the book down and begin to look around and start to practice what the creative force allows you to do. Simply, look at any object and imagine its beginning and all the steps necessary to create it. Also, start with any thought and repeat it multiple times. Then, describe what you see in your head. I know that this sounds a bit "eastern religion", but you must begin to see with your third eye, your brain.

For example, as an exercise, begin to repeat, "I am cleaning my house" and repeat it multiple times until you begin to see the image that appears in your brain. Practice this with your friends and you will begin to see that each one creates a unique picture in one's brain because our backgrounds are different.

Also, do not forget to post the signs described in the first chapter and continue to write the exercise prescribed for you to do.

CHAPTER FOUR

THE ENERGY OF A THOUGHT

Thus far, we have learned that there is a process of creation that begins with a picture in our heads that I have chosen to call thought. The process of creation is not really started by having a thought, but rather by the repetition of a thought. The consequence of repeating a thought is the creation of an energy that goes by many names, but in most cases it is called motivation. This motivation is not a generic motivation. It is very specific. Along with the motivation to do some actions, those actions are also very specific. As the consequence of repeating a particular thought, the brain sees the steps required for a person to take. Again, these steps required are not generic, they are very specific. The final destination in the process of creation is the consequence of the actions taken. The exciting and wondrous thing about this creative process is that the final result is identical to the thought with which you began. It is almost as if the thought jumps from one dimension and becomes a physical reality that we can sense, feel, and touch.

The first question that comes to mind is, "Why is it that not all the thoughts I think become reality?" The answer is rather simple for those of us who have a science background. We all have different amounts of energy. Energy is really the center point of creation and whether you are talking about the energy from the sun or the energy from a gallon of gas, it comes down to the fact that it is the same energy just in different forms. Therefore, if we pay attention to a thought such as, "I am making hamburgers tonight", it will require less energy, less effort, less time to create than if I begin to repeat, "I am going to be a doctor". I was five years old when I began to repeat it and I was 31 years old when I was officially able to work as a physician.

I experimented with thoughts and quickly realized that the energy in each thought must not be that much, or rather the energy required to create certain actions must be greater in the order of thousands of repetitions. To explain this point, I am going to use the example of a smoker. When a smoker first decides to light a cigarette, on an average day, the smoker usually repeats the thought, "I need a cigarette" probably about 100 times from the moment he initiates the process to the moment he lights the cigarette. It is a similar conversation that each one of us has with oneself on any issue. For discussion sake, let us assume that this smoker is age 56. Let us also assume that he began to smoke at age 16. Forty years have passed between the initiation of the habit to present time. If we assume that this particular smoker, smokes one pack a day, or 20 cigarettes a day, and he smokes 350 days of the year, the math becomes rather easy.

Number of repetitions from initial thought to action	100 times
Number of years smoking	40 years
20 cigarettes a day times 350 days a year	7000 cig/year.

This smoker, from the time he began to smoke to present time, has repeated the thought, "I need a cigarette" 28 million times. Therefore, the craving to smoke is going to be quite strong.

The amount of energy in one single thought is very tiny requiring an extensive repetition of a particular thought. If a non-smoking individual repeats, "I want a cigarette" 100 times, the energy generated would be minimal, not causing any changes in his behavior at that particular moment. I assume that this energy simply dissipates much like a spark coming out of a fire. However, as a scientist, I cannot assume that the energy created disappears because in physics classes I have learned that energy simply changes form.

Even though I gave this example to relate the amount of energy in each thought, it also helps to point out the existence of other forces at play. One of these forces is knowledge.

Knowledge is the accumulation of facts, but it is a rather weak force to change your behavior. The force created by your thinking, "the creative force" is extremely powerful and it will force your behavior. The creative force will force you to do even the things that you do not like or want to do, such as smoking. I want to make certain that you are clear that all the smokers in the world are well aware that smoking is a health hazard that causes cancer and that the amount of money burned smoking is staggering. The smoker possesses the knowledge that smoking is not good for health or pocket, yet the smoker appears unable to quit. If the smoker is only using the power of his/her knowledge to try to quit, it is obvious that knowledge is a very weak force to change behavior.

The power created by the repetition of thoughts, "the Creative Force" is therefore, proportional to the number of repetitions done, and the consequence created requires a specific number of repetitions. Let me use an example that would be easier to understand. Think of each thought as a penny. By the mere repetition of the thought, I am accumulating pennies, but the effect or consequence would depend on the purchase price I am required to pay to create a specific outcome.

I can use many metaphors to represent what a thought is. The one I like the most is to think of a thought like the spark or the amber that escapes from burning wood. We all have seen such burning objects. This small package of energy leaves the fire, travels a short distance, and quickly dies off losing all its energy. It is not that the energy was lost. The energy simply became heat and it was absorbed by the air surrounding it. Similar effects occur with all our thoughts. Therefore, every thought counts. However, the thoughts that you repeat the most are the ones that you become more aware in your reality.

The unit of this energy is the thought or the image that appears in one's head. I can repeat a thought simply by looking at an image over and over all the time. This creative process does not have to leave my brain to be effective. However, I can increase this energy by speaking the thought or by writing the thought. Considering that it takes more effort to speak what is on one's mind, the spoken word appears to be far more powerful than the mere image in one's brain. I have experimented with the writing of a specific thought and I have discovered that it takes more energy, more effort to write my thought than just speaking the thought.

Someone once said, "There is a great deal of power in looking at your goals written in your own handwriting". I will be the first one to tell you that I have not even attempted to measure this energy called thought, but since it is an energy it can be felt by mere repetition of the thought. For example, if I have the thought, "I am going to be a doctor", I could give this a value of 1 in this energy measurement. I suspect, and I am guessing that when I speak, "I am going to be a doctor" the energy measurement would likely be a 10. Let us assume that I decide to write this thought on a piece of paper. I sense that the power of writing the thought would be more like 100. Remember, that these are impressions created in my brain and that no measurement has been taken. This is a simple example given in order to explain how the energy of the thought can be increased by simple repetition.

This becomes more easily realized when you focus on the process of creation and use it in reverse. Let us assume that you enjoy chocolate in any form. If you put your liking of chocolate as an outcome, it is safe to assume that this outcome, as all other outcomes, was caused by some actions. The actions that led you to enjoy chocolate would have been the result of the repetition of a thought such as, "I love chocolate". This repetition could have been silent, spoken, or written. If you assume that you have repeated this thought for a long period of time, then it is safe to say that you have repeated that particular thought in the millions of times. The total number of repetitions have created a strong desire, a craving, to eat chocolate.

For discussion sake, imagine that you changed your mind and start to repeat, "I hate chocolate" and intentionally repeat it 100 times versus the millions of times that you have already said, "I love chocolate". The net effect would be expected to be insignificant. If you were to see a piece of chocolate candy, you would feel the creative force in the form of a craving, simply because you had been repeating, "I love chocolate" longer and a greater number of times.

Using the previous example, it is not shocking that when one repeats, "I hate chocolate" frequently, intentionally, and for a long period of time, whether one believes it or not, one would think twice before eating it. Furthermore, if one keeps repeating the thought, one day it will become true and one would hate chocolate. What one would realize is that one would be able to resist chocolate candy. The mere process of repetition creates the energy. This energy created by the creative process has a specific function. This energy will become physically real or become the physical form of the thought. In conclusion, the thought becomes your reality or stated in another form, the thought and the outcome are equal only for those thoughts that you repeat.

CHAPTER FIVE

MORE DETAILS ABOUT THE CREATIVE FORCE

THE CREATIVE FORCE

P R O C E S S

FIRST
YOU HAVE A THOUGHT
(Image in Your Brain)

SECOND
YOU REPEAT THE THOUGHT
(Speaking, Writing, Thinking)

THIRD
YOUR BRAIN SHOWS YOU THE STEPS/ACTIONS
(You become motivated to act.)

FOURTH
YOU CREATE YOUR REALITY OR OUTCOME
(The created result is identical to the original thought.)

It should be clear to you by now that there is an energy in our thinking. When the thought is repeated, it forces us to make some decisions, some actions which have as the unique consequence, the ability of creating the physical form of the thought. For example, if I begin to repeat, "I am making burgers tonight" and I choose to continue to repeat this particular thought, I can, by the use of the creative force, predict with certainty that, "I will be making burgers tonight". This is possible only because according to the creative force, the thought and the outcome are equal.

An important detail to mention, at this point, is that the following premise applies to all forces of nature and therefore, applies to this creative force. All forces in nature are neutral. I think a short explanation will suffice for you to begin seeing this basic, yet extremely important point. Let us take a force such as fire. When I control fire and make it small, under a pot with food, this fire is going to be providing me with a positive outcome; cooked food. On the other hand if I choose to set a forest on fire, the same force, yet out of control, would create a negative outcome.

Another analogy for this clarification is the use of electricity. If I used electricity to charge my phone, it would be considered positive because the energy or force called electricity allowed me to connect with and help other family members. Let us assume that I used electricity to make an electric chair in death row active. In this case, the same electricity has now empowered me to kill another human being, thus causing a negative outcome.

Whether we are talking about fire, electricity, or the Creative Force, I, the person using the force, determine the outcome. With the Creative Force, if I begin with a positive thought such as, "I love my children", the outcome produced would be positive. Now, let us imagine that I choose to repeat a negative thought like, "I hate my children" (not recommended), the expected outcome would be negative. In summary, who is responsible for creating the positive or negative outcome? The answer is rather simple: The thinker.

This simple, yet profound detail is so liberating because now when I find myself in the middle of a negative situation, I do not have to look outside of my brain to find the solution. The solution is already within me because I am the one in control of the thoughts I choose to repeat.

Switching details, in a previous chapter I asked you to think of the energy of the thought like a penny because we already have the concept of money in our minds. The positive thought could be like a penny you put in a savings account and a negative thought would be like a penny you spent that you didn't have to spend in the first place. Therefore, it stands true that the more one repeats a particular thought, the stronger the creative force is going to become, either positive or negative. This strength is not the only characteristic of thoughts that we need to understand.

During my lectures, a simple exercise that I ask from the audience is to repeat the thought, "I am cleaning my house". Now, I ask you, my reader, to do the same. Simply, repeat that particular thought in your head or with your spoken word as many as 20 times.

What surprises people and I assume you as well is the question that follows. What did you see in your head? Some will answer my bedroom, while others answer the kitchen, the yard, or garage. We all create an image when we repeat a thought and the image does not have to be the same. The conclusion that I hope you are able to make is that your brain transported your mind, yet your body remained in the same location. This should not be news to you. Our imagination makes us go to places where we have never been physically. That simple, yet profound observation brings us to see thoughts in another way: thoughts have direction.

In the introduction, I mentioned that when I discovered that thoughts have energy that can be manipulated, I was able to visualize how thoughts were making me move in different directions. I want you to imagine a road between two points. Let us call Point A thinness and point B fatness. It is safe to assume that we all begin in the middle, since at the beginning we are not aware of our body appearance. As a teen, I began to criticize my looks and every time I thought or said something negative, my brain was moved in the direction of fat. With the passage of time, the number of repetitions began to add up and in spite of my dislike and opposition, it kept me moving in that direction. It was almost as if I were being pushed from behind, yet I was not able to see what was pushing me. I certainly did not want to gain more weight, but I had no control over the problem. My lack of control was humiliating because it was in direct contrast to the knowledge I had accumulated from my medical studies. As I mentioned before, I was the fat doctor telling my patients to lose weight.

When I began to experiment with thought, I chose the thought, "I look great". I was definitely moved in the direction of thinness. I want you to take a second and visualize the first moment I said it. My physical body was still fat. Nothing on the outside had changed, only my thinking in the inside and no one could see my thoughts. The experiment that I set up was simple. What is going to happen if I repeat the thought? To my surprise and welfare, the more I repeated the thought the faster I was moving in the direction of thinness. A similar process is going to occur to you, the reader, when you change any thought. For example, if you have been repeating, "I am poor" and you begin to repeat, "I am wealthy", or if you are sick and begin to repeat, "I feel better and better" changes will occur. Remember, that at the beginning of the process, the only change that has taken place in your thinking is not visible to anyone else. However, be reassured that if you persist in the repetition, slowly your physical changes are going to become more noticeable to you and anyone else who surrounds you regardless of the thought you repeat.

To summarize, what we have learned so far; these little things that we call thoughts that we have been ignoring until now do have an appreciable energy that accumulate with repetition and they move us in the direction the thought is requesting. Unfortunately, that is not all you need to know about your thoughts.

Thoughts are very particular as to the effect they have. Due to the fact that each thought has a particular effect, it can be said that thoughts have fields or areas that they can affect. As an example, if I repeat, "I have great hair" and I choose to repeat it many times and over a long period of time, two things are going to happen.

My brain is going to see the steps to take to make my hair look great and I will feel the force or the motivation to act on those steps. The net result of my actions is guaranteed. My hair is going to look great because the thought and the outcome will be equal for the thoughts I choose to repeat. One observation to make at this point is that the thought, "I have great hair" is not going to help my financial picture. The reason is that the area or field of action of the thought, "I have great hair" is limited. My financial picture would be created by a different set of thoughts relating to money making and money saving. Now, If I choose to repeat, "I am wealthy" in addition to, "My hair looks great", the end result that people would see after repeating those thoughts for a long time would be a wealthy man with great looking hair.

Let us assume that I repeat, "I have no luck with women", in addition to the previous two thoughts. What people are going to see or what I am going to become will be a wealthy man, with great looking hair who has a series of failed relationships. Thus, keep in mind WHATEVER THOUGHT YOU REPEAT, YOU SHALL BECOME.

The area that a thought affects can be manipulated up or down depending on the effect that you want to change. For example, you are familiar with the thought, "I have great hair". The only area affected is going to be my hair. I can increase the size of the thought by repeating a larger thought such as, "I love my head". The reason is that the thought, "I love my head" would include my hair, my eyes, my teeth, my smile, and my neck. The area of the thought can be increased again if I change the thought, "I love my head" to "I look great today". The latter thought would include my looks from head to toe. I hope you can see how easily the size of the thought can be manipulated.

To add a little more strain to your brain, let us take the thought, "I look great today" and expand it by a variable called time. Therefore, if I change the word, "today" for another word such as, "all the time", the thought would become, "I look great all the time". This particular thought has now become an eternal thought by the simple addition of, "all the time". This and other eternal thoughts will become very important in the future chapters when we learn what thoughts we should be choosing to repeat.

Now, the bigger the thought or the size of the thought does not guarantee a good outcome. Bigger is not always better when it comes to thoughts. Choosing to reduce the size of a thought is at times a great advantage to your success.

Let us begin with the following scenario: I am a married man, but I am not aware of the consequences of my thinking. If I happen to repeat, "I like all women" and continually repeat this particular thought, my reality will be that I am going to be attracted to basically any female I see. This thought, of course, would make me very vulnerable to having affairs and being led away from faithfully loving my wife. From the fact that I know thoughts have consequences in this scenario, I have reduced the size of that particular thought field to include only my wife. My new thought has become, "I love my wife ONLY". By adding that

ONLY, I have restricted the field of that thought to be fulfilled only by my wife and no one else.

To review what we have learned about our thoughts, these little images, that appear in our brain, one must remember that they contain an energy that can be manipulated by mere repetition. Realizing the consequence of this energy should make us move in the direction of the destination that the thought determines. This forces us to become exactly what the thought described ever since the first time the thought was spoken.

CHAPTER SIX

THE MOST PROFOUND OBSERVATIONS

Soon after I became aware of the power of our thoughts; after I began to experiment with this energy; things began to appear very differently from the way I had seen those things in the past. Remember that I began to repeat, "I look great" and because I had become aware that I was calling myself fat, I simply flipped the thought. Until this point, I believed, as most of you believe now and what the rest of the world teaches, that obesity is created by too much food and very little exercise. I cannot really blame anyone for this type of thinking because of the existence of a force called knowledge. Knowledge teaches that if you are fat, it is because you eat too much and you do not exercise enough. The problem with the force called knowledge is that it is a very weak force to change our behavior. What one must realize is that our behavior is under control of another energy called the Creative Force which is the subject of this book.

As I began to repeat the thought, "I look great", my brain began to work in a different way. I felt a strong desire to stop eating carbohydrates. Therefore, I made a list and began to eliminate the most obvious carbs. The immediate result was the loss of 30 pounds in one month. I became aware that the thought, "I look great" was becoming my reality. As I continued to repeat the thought, my brain shifted to walking long distances; next came weight lifting; and recently I began making fruit and protein smoothies. Now, I simply continue to repeat the thought, "I look great". I repeat this with the confidence that my brain will show me the steps to take.

After that original thought, I expanded my research with many different thoughts. The first observation I made was that the thought itself will reveal to the brain only the steps that one must take in order to make the said thought a reality. The brain will not show one any other step. In addition to the steps to take, the brain will also provide the motivation to accomplish the said thought. It is almost as if the thought creates itself only.

I began teaching this method to my patients. I would teach them to call themselves beautiful and perfect. A pattern began to emerge. Those who were successful with losing the weight permanently were also the ones more committed to the repetition of the new thought. After interviewing those patients who were failing at weight loss, it became clear that they were having trouble with the repetition of positive thinking about their shape rather than their weight. Another light came on in my brain.

When a person becomes obese, that person complains not about their weight (a number), but about his/her shape. The pattern I noticed was that the obese person, did not like what they saw in the mirror; When they proposed to lose ten pounds and then sacrificially lost the ten pounds and saw themselves in the mirror, they did not like their shape in spite of the weight loss success. Consequently, the weight came back because their thought (the number) was not the thought that caused the weight problem.

Once I became aware that, in general, obese people complain about the shape of their bodies, I decided to turn it around and confirm my suspicion. I decided to interview many of my skinny patients simply to confirm what thoughts they expressed about their shape when they were in front of a mirror. Almost universally they expressed positive thinking. This affirmed my suspicion that if the thought is positive, the outcome is positive and if the thought is negative, the outcome is negative.

Even with this discovery, my inquisitive brain could not rest. I decided to go back and interview those patients who failed to lose weight and review the environment where they functioned in order to discover if their spouses were supportive or derogatory. To my surprise, I found that most of the women who had failed consistently heard positive things from their spouses, yet their own thinking was quite negative. The biggest truth about thinking became clear to me just as if an explosion occurred in my brain. The brain is only affected by the thinker's own thoughts. Another way to express it: Your brain only listens to your own personal voice.

I have a scientific mind and I do not accept anything that appears to be logical if it only occurs one time. My scientific mind requires repeat testing or further proof to see how universal that observation was. After several months of keen observation, it became clear to me that the energy of the thought has the limit of affecting only the person having and repeating the thought.

Many questions appeared in my brain as I began to apply these new insights to my daily life. One of those questions was, "Can a person control all the thoughts they repeat"? The moment the question appeared in my head, my brain yelled: "Only if you think so". In the conversation that followed in my brain, one side of my brain was saying , "What do you mean"? The other side was answering, "This question, like any question, could have multiple answers and the answer that you choose determines and becomes your reality".

For the question, "Can a person control all the thoughts he/she repeats?" the answers would lie between yes, of course, and not at all, with many possibilities in between. Due to my awareness that whatever thought I repeat becomes my reality, I have chosen, and I recommend that you choose, the answer: YES! Any person can control all of his/her thoughts and continually repeat that thought. Considering the size of the thought, this answer becomes an eternal thought with the addition of the ending, "all the time".

Remember, that the repetition of the thought reveals to your brain all the steps to take in order to make the thought become a reality. Therefore, I began to repeat, "Yes, I control all my thoughts, all the time". My brain revealed to me that I needed to create an environment where the repetition of the chosen thought occurs automatically, as in the examples mentioned in chapter one; the work that must be done.

Thus far, I have discussed that with this energy thoughts can accumulate; that this energy reveals the steps to take; that it gives the motivation to the thinker only; and that the thinker can control all thoughts if he or she so chooses. Of course, that was not the end of my brain asking questions. There was a lot more to learn. What about prayer? What about if I repeat, "I can change people"? What then?

To answer these questions, I wish to tell you that as soon as I became aware of the power of thinking, I wanted to teach it to the whole world. This book is one of the steps I have taken to achieve my new goal. Another step that I took five years ago was to use the process of the creative force to heal addiction. Then and there, it became obvious that the question, "can I change people?," needed to be answered. Just as before, my brain was yelling at me, "Well, that is a thought". What my brain was telling me was that the outcome depended only on the answer I choose to give. Therefore, if I answer "No, I cannot change people"; then that thought becomes my reality and my brain would not show any actions to take. Since not changing people requires no action on my part, that was not acceptable to me. The brain that I was blessed with chose to repeat, "Yes, I can all the time". This is a universal thought due to the fact that this thought has a huge field of action and an eternal duration.

Therefore, I began to repeat, "Yes, I can cure addiction. Yes, I can change and help people". My brain began to show me what to do. I lecture as a volunteer in an inpatient, 30 day long drug rehab program. It is the highlight of my week every Wednesday night. As I train people in the art of thinking correctly, I have discovered many similarities with Alcoholics Anonymous and Celebrate Recovery. It is very rewarding because my brain now sees with clarity the causes of addiction, what prolongs addiction, and the keys to the cure of addiction. During the meeting/lecture there are occasions of heated discussion because a few of the concepts are hard to accept for some of the addicts. What I have noticed, almost universally, is that my brain makes me sensitive when needed and tough when required. It is not difficult for me to say to an addict, "Quit feeling sorry for yourself". I know that when you are reading this book that statement sounds offensive to some but, to an addict, in the right circumstance, that statement could make the difference between life and death.

I often run into my Recovery in Process clients who universally tell me that my lectures changed their lives. My actions have the power to change other people's thinking, but it remains critical that the addict must change his/her thinking in order to change his/her life. My thinking, "I can change people", changed my actions, but my actions have the power to change the addicts' thinking where the origins of addiction are. AA says it like this: The addict must change his/her stinking thinking in order to change their reality.

I feel the need to summarize this chapter by repeating that, "The power of my thoughts is limited to the creation of what the thought describes and that my brain is synchronized to my own voice only".

CHAPTER SEVEN

REALITY

To briefly review what I have been teaching thus far, I have decided to introduce the banner I use when lecturing. From observing the banner, you can more easily understand the process of creation that I call the Creative Force. It begins with a thought; one must choose to repeat the thought; the thought causes one to do certain actions; and finally, the consequence of the actions, called outcome, occurs. The beauty of this process is that the image that the thought produced becomes physically real. Therefore, the thought and the outcome are said to be equal.

THE CREATIVE FORCE

FIRST
YOU HAVE A THOUGHT
(Image in Your Brain)

SECOND
YOU REPEAT THE THOUGHT
(Speaking, Writing, Thinking)

THIRD
YOUR BRAIN SHOWS YOU THE STEPS/ACTIONS
(You become motivated to act.)

FOURTH
YOU CREATE YOUR REALITY OR OUTCOME
(This created result is identical to the original thought.)

As a general example, if I state, "I am making a table" and I repeat that thought, the final consequence would be that I end up with a physical table. Now, that I have reviewed these simple statements, I want you to look around the room where you are. There is no need to move. If you see a chair, you can affirm that the chair began as a thought. If you see a framed photo, you could say that the framed photo began as a thought. If you see a rug, you could say that the rug began as a thought. If you see a lamp, you can say that the lamp began as a thought. The interesting point to make at this time is that you are surrounded by things that began as thoughts from different places and at different times. What brings these thoughts together is the fact that you are looking at those items at the same time and in the same place. One would refer to this state as your reality. Therefore, my reality or for that matter anyone's reality is very similar. It has been created by thoughts from yourself and from other people, but you are experiencing them all at the same time and in the same place.

Why not complicate the situation a little bit? Imagine that if one began to repeat a long time ago thoughts such as, "I am a millionaire" and "I hate pizza". The reality that one would experience is formed by some thoughts that already have become a physical reality. Thoughts such as, "I hate pizza" that you cannot see, but have become reality and finally, some thoughts such as, "I am a millionaire" which have not become truth, but are in the process of creation.

The good news about realities, yours or mine, is that they can be easily changed by altering the thoughts that created them. It is as if they are plastic or rather evolving states of energy traveling through time and space. The realities that we experience are not fixed in stone. All realities can be changed.

I want you to think for a moment about your own thoughts. You may have grown up in a politically Democratic home. While in college, you chose to join the Republican Party. As time passed, you felt betrayed by the Republican Party, so now you think of yourself as an Independent. Your view of reality changed because you have been changing your thoughts. When you were a Democrat, you felt victimized by the wealthy; as a Republican you felt the workers were lazy and wanted more than they deserved; and as an Independent you may have a more balanced view of reality. It is your choice to think of a reality as good or bad, hopeful or hopeless. Your experience of reality does not depend on the chairs, nor the tables and lamps. The perception of reality depends on how you choose to view that specific reality at the moment you chose to experience the said reality. In order to better explain realities, I want you to imagine a big fancy home filled with rich and expensive furnishings. Inside this house lives a man who repeats a thought such as, "I hate everyone". Due to this negative thinking, he would see his reality as a mean, cold, and unfriendly place, regardless of the fine house and furnishings. Now, imagine a modest home with worn furnishings where there is a mother who repeats a thought such as, "God gave me the best family ever". Her reality would feel more like heaven on earth because her thinking allows her to experience the reality with a greater degree of happiness than what the physical surroundings would suggest.

In order to explain this simple, yet profound concept I was allowed to make another observation. I work and live in a small town in Western Kentucky surrounded by farms and lakes, rivers and woods. Nature at its best, very pretty. There are, however, some people in my area who complain about the small town and backward people who surround us. I recall one time that one of those people felt that they needed a big city such as New York where the cool people live; where life happens; and where life is exciting. This person paid $200 a night for a hotel room while in New York. At about that same time, I decided to hike the many trails available in the Land Between the Lakes Park. I ran into a couple from New York. Somehow during our conversation, it was mentioned that they were paying $200 dollars a night at a hotel by the lake in order to escape the lights, noise, and crowds to enjoy nature at its best. The couple from New York and I shared the same thought and therefore, we were able to see our surroundings in the same manner. This was unlike the local person who needed to see New York City. The point to understand is that our reality changes depending on the thoughts we choose to repeat.

One unique characteristic of thoughts is that thoughts can be added to a reality, even if the reality is not sensed by the same person. Imagine the couple from New York walking in The Land Between the Lakes. Now, imagine that the man was super excited to be there. Now, add to it the thought, the idea that the spouse was also super excited to be there. Once again, the experience of their reality would allow them to sense this reality at a higher level of satisfaction. Also, imagine that the husband was super excited, but the wife was there only for moral support. The man's experience would be lowered from the originally described situation because the energy derived from the wife's thinking and enjoyment would be subtracted from the whole experience.

Now, let us imagine a family of four agreed on a particular vacation site and all four are excited about taking this trip. The energy of their reality would achieve a higher plane of satisfaction because the addition of the positive energy is produced by every individual in their group.

Realities are not created by a single thought. Realities are created by multiple thoughts, even if the thoughts are not immediately observable. One of these examples would be the reality called addiction. Addiction is not created by someone saying, "I want to be an addict" or at least no addict has ever admitted that to me. Addiction is the result of multiple thoughts that come together to affect one person, all at the same time. Some of those thoughts are easily seen and noted. A common thought among addicts is, "I do not care", "life is hard", "there is no hope", etc. The practical application of this chapter is to point out to you that in order to change your reality you must begin by changing the thoughts that created that reality. The more thoughts you change, the more your reality is going to change.

To conclude, simply keep in mind that our personal reality is dictated by our thinking and our thinking is absolutely, 100% under our control. We must decide what thoughts to repeat all the time.

CHAPTER EIGHT

THE CARDENAS LAW

Ephesians 6:12 teaches us that our struggles are not against flesh and blood, but against powers and principalities...... One of these powers that causes confusion in our lives is the power of knowledge. It is always interesting to me that in the Garden of Eden there were two trees in the center of the garden; the tree of life and the tree of knowledge. The warning that God gave to mankind was that if one ate from the tree of knowledge, knowing right and wrong, one would surely die.

Growing up, the power of knowledge was mentioned in multiple ways by my parents, especially my mother who felt that education was the way to success. The power of knowledge appeared to be the key to solving all our problems, or is it? For most of my life, I have chased knowledge with an intensity, not commonly seen. I always felt the hunger to know more, or at least to know more than any other person near me. I have always felt capable of understanding even the more difficult subjects simply for the challenge of it. For example, while in college when most of my friends wanted to graduate with one major, my brain was only satisfied with two. Therefore, I studied to obtain a major in chemistry and a second in biology. In medical school, I also accumulated a great deal of knowledge - anatomy, physiology, biochemistry, pathology, surgery, pharmacology, etc. My brain was, is, and will continue to be a beautiful hard drive to store information.

Fifteen years ago, I found myself having to solve the biggest problem I had at that time, my obesity. I had become the fat doctor having to tell my patients to lose weight. Yet, I was unable to do it myself. Please keep in mind that my brain was, and is, full of knowledge. My brain knew what to do, but my brain was lacking the motivation to start doing it. There would be an occasional spurt, like a burst of energy, only to quickly return to the old habits. I ate brownies at night while watching television in spite of an uncomfortable sensation of fullness and despite having heartburn. It was insane. By morning after remembering the brownie eating, I would promise myself to change, only to repeat it night after night. I felt like a prisoner of my destiny, like a mad man, knowing what I wanted, and yet not knowing how to get it. I was paralyzed by a force that I could not see.

It became clear that all my knowledge, accumulated through the years, was not strong enough to change my behaviors. Please understand that it was not the lack of attempting to lose weight. It was that time after time, I failed to achieve the goal of normal weight in the same manner that many people are failing. My problem was that I was relying on the power of knowledge, yet the power of knowledge was a weak force to change my behavior. My behaviors are under the control of a more powerful force that I call the Creative Force. This book is exclusively intended to teach you that you are empowered with this force and my job is rather simple: to train you in how to use this force to your advantage.

The Creative Force has four steps: **thought, repetition, actions/behaviors, and outcome**. The Creative Force is limited to the thought itself. The Creative Force cannot create anything outside what the thought itself requests.

I began to experiment with this force 15 years ago and as I have mentioned earlier, my experiment was rather simple. I chose to search for any changes or consequences of the repetition of a particular thought. My initial thought was, "I look great" which was in direct contrast to the thought, "I am fat". After only a few repetitions, I began to sense the energy of the Creative Force; that in this case, you would call motivation. The first action I took was to make a list of food that I considered toxic to my body. Starches and sugars had to go, including the beloved brownies. To my surprise, I found it very easy to do; no struggle. As the weight began to come off, the motivation to walk long distances came to me, more as if a need to walk long distances entered my brain. The next action was to lift weights and as of lately I was motivated to add protein shakes to my diet. The consequences of all of those actions were that my body changed in shape and size and my body continues to move in the direction that my thought determined.

An interesting observation to make is that all the steps taken in my trip to, "I look great" are the same steps my knowledge knew I had to take, but the big difference was that the motivation to pursue those actions was given to me for free. The thought itself was forcing me down the road in the direction of, "I look great". I still wake about five o'clock in the morning fully rested with the desire to do some exercise and the craving to prepare my protein shake. It is so ingrained in my brain that the days that my work prevents me from exercising, I feel a discomfort, a need to use my muscles in the same manner as if working out. The observation to keep in mind here is that my behaviors are under the control of the Creative Force and not under the control of the power of knowledge.

For the sake of completeness, I need to mention that knowledge and the Creative Force are not the only forces affecting your life. Fear, hate, love, accountability, authority, etc. are other forces, but they are relatively as weak as knowledge to change your behavior.

The next logical question in my brain was of course, how is it that this force controls my behavior? The explanation is rather simple: It follows the CARDENAS LAW. The CARDENAS LAW is not a new force or power. It is the mere description of how the Creative Force controls our behavior.

In the simplest way to express it is that, "Our brain only shows us the actions that complete the thought we are repeating the most". It has as its function to fulfill the thought or to complete the thought. It is the vehicle used by the thought to travel across dimensions so it becomes a physical reality. It is counter to the logic working with knowledge, but it is logical to the thought. A longer explanation is required in order for one to understand this powerful point.

I will begin with the thought, "I am fat". By now, anyone who is reading this book should be able to predict the outcome. Since you already know that the thought and the outcome are equal, you could predict that the person repeating the thought, "I am fat" is going to gain weight and become fatter. The repetition of this thought would eventually bring the thinker to a moment of choice when the behavior is to take place. Please do not rush to answer the question. Before I give the choices of behavior, you must answer the question, which choice completes or fulfills the thought? Remember, that the question is not, what should you do? (using knowledge) But rather, what choice completes the thought?

If I have been repeating the thought, "I am fat" and when the time comes to make a choice of food between the brownie or an apple, which choice completes or fulfills the thought, "I am fat"? The answer is of course, the brownie. Therefore, the thinker feels an incredible desire to choose the brownie and to dislike the apple. That desire to eat the brownie has been created by the repetition of the thought, "I am fat" and it is going to overrule any knowledge I might have in terms of being healthy or not. What happens when I choose the brownie? The thought becomes fulfilled and the thinker gains weight. Remember the CARDENAS LAW: Your brain will choose the choice that completes the thought.

Consequently, I gained weight because I ate the brownie. My slacks did not fit which led me to repeat, "I am fat" creating a vicious cycle. Now, imagine that I have to choose activities to do after dinner and I am presented with the choice of going for a walk versus watching television. Remember, that the question is, what choice completes the thought, "I am fat"? It is not what you should do? The latter is based on knowledge. The thinker is going to feel an incredible need to sit down and watch television while making excuses why walking is not a good idea at that moment. Why did the thinker choose the television versus the walking? The answer is that the television choice fulfills or completes the thought, "I am fat". This behavior can be predicted in advance by the use of the CARDENAS LAW.

The thought, "I am fat" when repeated, creates a force that makes the thinker choose the brownie and the television activity as the only choices possible, making the thinker choose them. The consequence of those choices is of course that the thinker gains weight, thus making the thought, "I am fat" become a reality. The person doing the repetition has the knowledge of what is healthy and good for him/her to lose weight, but the knowledge is too weak of a force to direct his/her behavior. One's behavior, all our behaviors, are under the control of the Creative Force, generated by all the thoughts that we have been repeating since we were able to think.

Another example is needed in order to clarify any doubts in your mind. I changed my thinking during my experiment from, "I am fat" to "I look great". I began to repeat it intentionally and often. I have never attempted to count the number of times a particular thought should be repeated, but I began to repeat it as part of the experimentation with this energy. I remember that the first thing I did was to make a list of foods I was going to avoid. As I continued to repeat, "I look great", I felt an energy, a motivation, almost an assurance that I was going to be able to accomplish something new. As I was given the food choice between the brownie or the apple, my choices began to change.

Remember that the question to answer is not, what should you do, but rather, which choice completes the new thought? The answer in this case, for this thought and for this choice, would be the apple. What I then felt was a craving for the apple and a distaste for the brownie. It was a rather simple choice because the brownie had lost its allure.

After the first month when I lost 30 pounds, the excitement was building and the repetition increased. The next step was an incredible desire for physical activity. Consequently, when I was presented with the choice between watching television versus walking, the choice became easier. The reason was because the CARDENAS LAW was at work. Walking, simply completed the thought, "I look great".

I know that at this point you may not realize the power of this teaching, but in the months that followed, my brain began to question every thought that I had been repeating causing me to appreciate the power of thoughts. With the awareness that all things begin with a thought and if I repeat a particular thought, the energy generated dictated my action. The consequences that those actions were predictable gave me a sense of control over my life. I realized my life was controlled by my thoughts and I was the responsible party for the thoughts I chose to repeat. I began to find the explanation for why becoming a physician was rather easy; saving money was rather easy; and losing weight was now rather easy and logical.

While in the dark periods of my life, before my enlightenment of the Creative Force, my efforts were directed to managing my behaviors. After the enlightenment, my focus became laser sharp and I began to focus exclusively on managing my thoughts. The reason was because once you become aware of the CARDENAS LAW, you realize that your behaviors, all your behaviors, are caused by your thinking. At that point, my life became logical not due to knowledge, but logical due to the Creative Force.

The simplicity of life can be summarized in the following statement:

> If your thought is negative and you repeat it, your action will be negative (mistake)

> and the result will be negative, BUT,

if the thought is positive and you repeat it, your action will be positive (correct action)

and the result will be positive.

Thus, in conclusion, I like to recommend that you stop worrying about your's and other people's behaviors and begin to pay attention exclusively to what we all are thinking.

CHAPTER NINE

YOUR PERSONAL REALITY

Inventory time: Now, that you have become aware that absolutely all of us humans have the power to think, you realize that we all possess the ability to generate this Creative Force. In addition, you are also aware that the Creative Force is at work whether you like it or not. Due to the fact that you are aware that your thoughts have consequences, it is time for each of us to take a long and deep look at ourselves and our thinking. We need to understand why things are the way they are. If you are like most humans, I suspect your life is a mixture of sweet experiences and others that are not very sweet. It is time to start analyzing every thought that has ever come out of your mouth. Each of those spoken thoughts may have already become true or are in the process of creation and each particular thought is about to give you some consequences that you may wish to avoid.

In the course of your life here on Earth, you may have spoken thoughts such as, "It is in God's hands", "There is no God", "I have no luck", " I like this or that", "I hate strawberries", etc, etc. Think back to as many of the thoughts as you can since you were a child and thoughts that you may have changed that you should not have changed. In addition, think of the thoughts that you have not begun to say that you should be repeating each day in order to create your future reality in a more positive way. Every thought must come under scrutiny and be given the OK to continue to be repeated or rejected, once and for all. This scrutiny should be done in order to carefully determine the merit of each thought to produce the most favor for you, your family, and the rest of the world. This should be done in a manner that would not adversely affect or leave any area of your purpose in life unchecked.

We must all begin the work required in analyzing our present reality and to break it down through the process of the Creative Force. We must be able to identify the thoughts that are being repeated in order to identify the good ones from the not so good thoughts. In order to accomplish this task, I recommend you use a mirror, not a physical mirror, but one you can create with your thoughts. You are to place yourself between the said mirror and the imagined object in front of the mirror. Next, imagine that the mirror is to your left and you can see it easily; and to the right is the object that the mirror is reflecting, your outcome. The image of the object in the mirror would be your thought and the object to the right of you is the outcome or reality that the thought created. At this point, this exercise should be rather easy because by now you are an expert in the Creative Force. Consequently, you clearly know that the thought and the outcome are equal.

Let us assume you look to the right and you see the outcome, a physician. Without looking to the left, you should be able to predict that in the past you must have been repeating, "I am going to be a doctor". Once again, this is possible because the Creative Force told you that the only outcome possible after repeating, "I am going to be a doctor" would be a doctor just as you saw that image in your brain. If you look to the right and you see a fat person, you can predict that in the past negative thoughts describing your looks were used to describe the image you saw. Again, thought and outcome are equal.

Changing course, I am now going to ask you to turn your head toward the mirror and without moving your head, I want you to predict your future outcome with different thoughts. This is possible because you know the thought and the outcome are predictably equal as the Creative Force dictates. First, turn to the left and in the mirror you read the thought, "Life is hard" and repeat this thought for a long time. You should be able to predict, using the CARDENAS LAW, that in your future you are going to make some mistakes and the result of those mistakes is that your life is going to be harder than it is now. Your life is going to become harder, not because life will be harder for everyone else, but because you are the one and only one affected by your thinking. Now, the question you must ask is should I continue to repeat this simple thought or should I change it? Your answer might be, "Yes", "No", " I do not know" or "No one knows what the future will bring". That is another thought and therefore, must be asked in front of the mirror.

You should look to the left where the mirror is and you see the thought, "No one knows the future", a very common thought. Since you understand the Creative Force, you can predict that if I repeat, "No one knows the future" the outcome or your reality would include

UNCERTAINTY. Again, this reality would apply only to you and no one else since your thoughts only affect you, the thinker.

The number of negative thoughts that we repeat without the knowledge of the Creative Force is huge and unless we become aware of all of them, we might be creating a great degree of difficulty for ourselves. Thinking that it is our destiny (no control) rather than our creation (all under our control) is dangerous.

One example of such thoughts that I hear frequently in my practice is, "I am getting old" or "We all are getting old". I must warn you not to repeat either of those thoughts and I will explain why. Imagine that you look to the left of the mirror and you read the thought, "I am getting old". Based on all your knowledge of the Creative Force and the infallibility of its force, you can predict that the person to the right is going to be aged, possibly with osteoporosis, with a walker, and shuffling down the hallway in a nursing home. Also, the CARDENAS LAW allows you to predict some of the behaviors that you would see that caused the person to the right to become feeble. The CARDENAS LAW allows you to understand that the thinker would not be likely to exercise, or to avoid cigarettes, or to refrain from any other harmful behaviors. The loss of health occurs because the choice of behavior is dictated by the thought itself. The thought, "I am getting old" is going to be fulfilled even if one does not like the consequence.

In addition to the activities described in the first chapter, that should be becoming part of your DNA, I recommend that you spend a considerable amount of time with the mirror activity. It must become second nature to you in order to explain how you have arrived at your current location and set of circumstances. You will be able to appreciate where you are (explaining the past thinking) and more importantly, how you are going to get where you want to be in the future (new thinking).

One of the observations that I have made when I lecture is that the listener sometimes expresses a thought as if it is the most common sense law ever written. My answer is generally taken as being sarcastic or rather that it sounds sarcastic, but that was not my intention. I simply answer, "That is a thought". The listener believes and affirms his/her thought by the way he/she lives based on the thought he/she has been repeating. You, as the reader, are going to find yourself questioning some "Truths" with which you have lived. I want to encourage you to question your every thought because the explanation given by the Creative Force is going to be far simpler than you can ever imagine and allow more peace in your life.

One such situation I found myself in was when I commented on the expression, "The rich get richer and the poor get poorer". First, I want you know that in the past I have made the same statement. I remember that the person who made that comment on that occasion was referring to what they saw as a conspiracy between the wealthy and the government to keep the masses down. That person saw an unbreakable ceiling that prevented him from achieving a significant form of success. Consequently with the repetition of that thought, the listener was creating the ceiling barrier. The listener was the one creating the conspiracy which limited his efforts. The listener had accepted that nothing was going to change. Therefore when he repeated those thoughts, he created a reality of hopelessness and anger. Do not let the same thing happen to you!

The explanation given by applying the Creative Force is rather simple. The wealthy person repeats the thought, "I can make a lot of money" and so he does. The CARDENAS LAW predicts that the wealthy person is going to be spending his/her time thinking of ways to make and save more money. There is not a need to look for a conspiracy. The poor person who spends his day thinking how difficult it is to make money and how difficult it is to save money creates walls and obstructions in his mind. With his thoughts, the final outcome is going to be that he will end up poorer than he was when he began having those thoughts. Yes, the rich get richer because of their thinking and the poor get poorer because of their thinking.

A nail in the coffin: Bill Gates went from poor to billionaire because of the thought, "Yes, I can".

CHAPTER TEN

THE DISCOVERY OF TIME AND THE APPLICATION OF SIZE

As stated in the previous chapter, I decided to ponder the thoughts I was thinking. I felt excitement because I had several weapons on my side. First, I understood that all things are created by thought. I understood that the repetition of a thought would create an energy that I chose to call the Creative Force. I understood that my brain was synchronized to my voice only. I understood that this force has the limitation of creating exactly what the thought describes. I understood that no matter how many people wished something on me, I was the one responsible for repeating the thought required to create my outcome. I must say that I felt on top of the world. My weight was coming off, my body shape was changing due to the fact that I was analyzing every thought that I had been repeating. Progress was happening.

Since I was aware of the mirror exercise, I only had to imagine my future. I then created thoughts that would produce that future; the rest was repetition. I have never been a socialist, someone who wants everyone to have the same. In that manner, I have always been more competitive. I want more than most and I am willing to do the work for it. I decided to obtain wisdom, strength, health, wealth, valor, and fearlessness; literally, I wanted it all. Hence, my initial thought was, "I will be wise, kind, meek, strong, healthy, wealthy, and fearless." I made signs and placed them in places where my brain would see them, and I began to repeat that thought. I even made a recording of my voice on an MP3 file and played it over and over. I was listening to my own voice repeat the thought.

After a few days of repetition, I came to realize that the mirror is right, but my thoughts contained an element of time that affected the outcome. For example, if I repeat, "I am making burgers tonight", the thought itself sets the limit to hamburgers tonight and nothing else. I could express the thought, "I am making burgers this week" or I can repeat, "I am having burgers for lunch". The thought itself appears to contain control of time. When I began to repeat, "I am going to be a doctor", the image created already contained a time factor because the image was one of an adult in his 30's. The image was not a doctor such as young Doogie Howser, MD. Whether expressed intentionally or not, all thoughts have a time factor, a determinant, a variable of time. When I began to repeat the thought, "I will be wise, kind, meek...", I was pushing time forward to a later period. I was prolonging the time when it, the thought, was going to become my reality. What was becoming more and more clear was that the thought also has the power to control time. Most of us, average humans, see time in a linear fashion and the idea of moving time backward does not seem possible. However, to some of us who have the pleasure of understanding quantum mechanics understand that time is relative, much like space and speed. The idea that I can control time with my thoughts was exciting to say the least. In a practical sense, my brain began to wonder and I began to question if I could become younger.

It still feels sarcastic when I answer, "That is a thought". I want you to understand that the question is not the thought, but the original point of thoughts where many answers begin. Most people live with the thought, "No, I cannot change time", but imagine that one chose to answer that question with the thought, "Yes, I can change time". All I will have to do is to begin repeating it and the CARDENAS LAW predicts that one's brain is going to show one the steps required to make this and any other thought become that person's reality.

A side note: questions are not thoughts, but rather the point where many thoughts can begin.

I had to rewrite my thought to: "**Today**, I am wise, kind, meek, strong, healthy, wealthy, and fearless". I have no doubt that I received all of these things, fairly quickly. The reason I can say that I received all of these things is because my brain began to see the world differently. This is really not a surprise, considering that I have told you that your reality changes when your thinking changes.

The next point in my progress was to become more keenly aware of the size of my thoughts and the effect of my thoughts on others. First, let me deal with the size of the thoughts first. When I repeat the thought, "There is nothing I can do", the field of this thought would not allow me to try anything. One could call this thought size zero when it comes to my ability. I can change the thought to, "I can do five things". You would then be able to tell that the size, the effect of this thought, would be bigger than zero. Next, I can change the thought to, "I can do all things". The size of this thought is much larger than the first two and yet, I can add time to those and make its field even bigger. For example, if I replace the old thought with, "I can do all things all the time" then, that thought becomes an eternal thought, meaning that this particular thought does not have limits. This thought became a much larger and more encompassing one.

It was at this time when I decided to enlarge my thoughts. I "Opened" my thoughts by adding the "-er" ending to the previous thoughts I had repeated. My new repetition became, "**Today**, I am wiser, kinder, meeker, stronger, thinner, healthier, wealthier, and fearless". The number of repetitions was then up to me. Remember, there is no one else responsible for repeating the thoughts, but you. You are 100% responsible for the thoughts you choose to repeat.

As I continued on the road to success in every field, I began to question the effect of my thoughts on other people. As you are aware, I taught you that your brain only listens to your voice and that remains true. I began to ponder how it is that prayer works and how it is that I can influence other people, or can I?

One common thought among those who have family members suffering addiction is, "The addict has to want sobriety" or "There is nothing you can do". When one repeats either of those thoughts, one causes inaction on one's part because the thoughts are simply not requiring change. Let us assume for a second that I changed the thought to, "I can cure any addict". Does it become my reality? The answer is yes, any thought that one repeats is going to create the desired reality. I decided to repeat the thought, "I can cure any addict". The desire to help those suffering from addiction appeared in my brain. The opportunity to do came to me through one of my patients. Soon, I was teaching the Creative Force on a weekly basis to addicts in a group rehabilitation center. It was not until I opened the door to the possibility, that the possibility occurred. As I lecture, I have noted my ability to change their thinking. My thoughts caused my actions and my actions changed their thinking. Once, the addicts recognize that their reality has been caused by their thinking, the solution to the problem of addiction comes fast and easy.

The change in the addicts' minds does not occur immediately; it occurs over a period of time as the new thinking begins to take effect and the stinking thinking begins to go away. When more negative thoughts are discarded and replaced with positive thoughts, the faster the recovery occurs. One of the most powerful tools to cause change in another person is to hold the other person accountable to the new thinking. To achieve the desired behavior, new thoughts must occur and those thoughts must be repeated. Accountability is a powerful force to change a person's thinking. When a person's thinking changes, so will their reality change.

CHAPTER ELEVEN

MY DISAPPOINTMENT

After my discovery of this energy that I termed the Creative Force and when I learned that all things begin as a thought, I started questioning every thought that I had been repeating. I recognized, for example, that since I was a child I had been repeating, "I am going to be a doctor" and the repetition of that thought had a major impact in my life. As a result of that repetition, I have felt the direction and purpose for my life. I also began to understand that thoughts such as, "I am fat" led to the negative portions of my life. However, thoughts, such as those, led me to identify the power of thinking and to recognize the different fields each thought affected.

As a result of repeating, "I am fat", I became fat in spite of all my knowledge. That thought created incredible difficulty in my life. I began to recognize how some people become successful and others do not. I began to understand how it is possible that one person could achieve huge success in one area of his/her life and total failure in other areas. I concluded that from that moment forward I was going to be evaluating every thought that I had received and repeated since I was a child. I was going to test all expressions, truths, and facts that I had ever heard. I was going to simply stick with the ones that the mirror exercise would approve; those thoughts that I would accept were in fact good ones.

I felt, to say the least, on top of the world. As I continued my repetition of my thoughts, I came to the realization that not very many people understood the power of thinking and the process of creation. I became intolerant of politicians and the news and felt attracted to deeper, wiser, bigger, and better thoughts. One night about 2 a.m. I woke and could not go back to sleep. I opened my Bible and I began to read Matthew, chapter 15. As I progressed in that story, I came to verse 19 and there it was. For those who are not familiar with Matthew 15:19, it states:

"For out of our heart proceeds evil thoughts..."

I was immediately disappointed that the things I had discovered as I studied thinking were in a book that was written 4,000 years ago. The disappointment did not last very long since I felt a fear that I was competing with God. I had learned through the years that you do not mess with God. I was happy to accept my place below God in His chain of command. My interest in the Bible teachings grew as my anger grew toward the Bible teachers in my past. After 45 years of hearing about God, did someone not know; could someone not have told me; could someone not have explained it to me? Why did someone not tell me that it was my thoughts that had caused my failures. Apparently, all of those nuns, pastors, and Bible teachers did not understand that my thinking was the cause of all my problems. I had come to that conclusion before I diligently began studying the Bible. To some degree, I felt confirmation of my new thinking. I felt assured that I was not the Lone Ranger with this wild idea that thoughts have energy and that energy has consequences.

Therefore, my interest in the teachings of the Bible grew even more. Before I dig more deeply into this matter, I want to point out that there are many things that up to this point still do not make sense. For example, God failed to save my nephew in spite of my constant prayer. After losing weight, I felt judgmental toward fat pastors. I judged pastors who were having extra marital affairs. It appeared to me that in each of those cases that God seemed to be out of reach, out of power, or incapable.

I want to introduce a disclaimer here. This book is about thinking and throughout this book, I hope to train you in thinking. I simply want to express my walk as I remember it. Also, I want you to appreciate that during my walk, my thinking has been changing and I suspect it will continue to change. This book is not intended to convince you to become a believer in Jesus Christ as presented by any specific church worker has done along your pathway. I have to admit, however, that my faith has increased to heights I did not imagine this would have been possible. My understanding of God, as the Bible explains Him has increased. After learning the Creative Force and reading what the Bible teaches, I feel I am growing closer to my Creator and the wonder of His love.

It was a bitter sweet feeling as I began to use the concordance Bible to search for the location of where my mind was wondering. I came to Proverbs 23:7 and there it was again, "as the man thinks, he becomes". This was exactly what I had concluded; we are the consequence of our thoughts. As the proof began to appear in the Bible, I became emboldened to continue teaching, for I felt I had back-up. I began to teach the 4 steps: **Thought**, **Repetition**, **Actions**, and the **Outcome**. Other names can be used, but the idea of the process remains the same. For those of you with a master's degree in business, you are taught the same process by the names: **Vision**, **Mission Statement**, **Action Plan**, and **Results**.

I remember reading the first Psalm. I have to give a pass, as an excuse, to the average person because the Bible that is accessible to us is very poetic. The King James version is hard to read while the NIV translates some of the poetry. When I, an average reader, read the first Psalm, I found myself confused, missing the most important points. Allow me the freedom of removing some of the poetry from it:

Psalm 1: 1-2a, Blessed is the man who
chooses to avoid the thoughts from
the wicked, but instead
chooses the thoughts from God.   **THOUGHT**

Psalm 1:2b... He meditates on it,
day and night   **REPETITION**

Psalm 1:3a... whatever he does, **ACTION**

Psalm 1:3b... prospers.   **OUTCOME**

At this point, I was becoming convinced of the need to continue my search for answers using the Bible more directly, not driven by blind faith, but rather armed with the knowledge of the Creative Force.

My initial pride of recognizing the power of thoughts and thus the Creative Force continued to be eroded by my continued reading of the Bible. I was able to recognize the process of the Creative Force in Psalm one, but it became rather easy to see in Joshua 1:8. Joshua is a book in the Old Testament that I had heard about, but I have to admit I had never paid much attention. My process of learning Bible truths really was limited to knowing a few verses that are familiar to most Christians, but by no stretch of anyone's imagination could I claim to know the Bible. Joshua 1:8 has the 4 steps in the process without much poetry, so it is easier to see without taking too much literary freedom. It reads:

> This book's instructions must not
> depart from your mouth;   **THOUGHT**
>
> you are to recite it day and night,   **REPEAT**
>
> that you may be careful to do
> everything written in it.   **ACTION**
>
> For then you will prosper and
> succeed in everything you do.   **OUTCOME**

By now, I had given up the idea that somehow I had discovered or had become aware of something new, but rather something that has been known for at least 4,000 years. Again, I do not wish to argue Christianity or the Bible. I am simply teaching you about thinking and the force created by its repetition. The fact that I found it written in the Bible only opened my mind to continue searching in that direction.

The Bible does say that the thoughts of God written or contained within the book are the keys to success in life. It also warns that our own personal thinking seems to lead to failure. As in the example given in James 1:13-15, it is revealed that God is immune to temptation and He is not in the business of tempting anyone. It points out that we are drawn by our human, negative **thinking** which when **repeated** leads to lust (a form of the Creative Force), which leads to sin (negative **action**) and terminates in death (a negative **outcome**).

In a more practical manner, I decided to observe if it was true that those who repeated the thoughts of God were more successful than those who did not. As I began to observe my mother's generation and then my own siblings, the pattern that evolved was quite clear that those who were reared with a strong faith-based family were more successful than those who were not.

If you expand your view and look around for those families where the children have followed the straight and narrow path to success, there seems to have been a strong faith-based influence. When one expands his/her observations to the opposite side of the spectrum, one finds that almost as universal law that with the lack of faith, there are people suffering from addiction. At this point, it is good to remind you, the reader, that there is a difference between knowing about God and repeating the thoughts of God. Most addicts that I come in contact with have had some religious training and KNOW some of the Bible verses, but do not understand their meaning. I am referring to the repetition of the thoughts that generate the force that makes one behave in a manner that leads to bad consequences. It is my experience that most addicts do not follow the thoughts that are taught in the Bible. The consequence of their thinking seems to be a very real suffering much like a hell of their own creation. I hope I do not have to remind you of the high mortality that surrounds drug addiction, but it would be logical to say that our thinking apart from God's thinking seems to lead to a physical death faster than the average as it is in the case of addicted people.

In order to connect you to my brain, I had to recognize that the power of thoughts and the Creative Force I had found, had also been written in the Bible some 4000 years ago. I had successfully experienced some of the Bible's claims. I had discovered that if you repeat the thoughts of the Bible, positive outcomes were promised and experienced. If you repeat your own thinking (without regard to God), the results were rather poor. This negative experience was not only spiritual, but rather a physical reality much like addiction and my obesity. I do not know if you see the next step, but in my brain it is very clear. I will begin dissecting the thoughts of God and the Bible to understand why they seem to be correct or rather preferable to my own thinking.

CHAPTER TWELVE

A FEW BIBLE VERSES

After becoming convinced of the power of thoughts and the process of creation, i.e. the Creative Force, and adding to the simple fact that I had found it in the Bible, it was time for me to continue my process of discovery.

I was attracted first to the verses of love. I read about thoughts related to love from the concordance Bible. Of course, I found plenty of them. If you take the thought, "Love one another", you find that the simplicity of this thought gives the appropriate field of action. It does not contain any limits. The thought does not say, "When it is easy", "When they are nice" or "If they deserve it". The thought itself suggests no limits. It is confirmed by multiple other references such as, "Love your enemies". Extensions of this thought also include, "Serve one another".

In contrast to the thoughts about love found in the Bible, you will also find thoughts warning you against self love and self preservation. If you begin to have conversation with any other person, you will find that we all operate based on thinking that is clearly too small in the field of love. The smallest field is, of course, "Self". If you function under the thought, "It is every man for himself", you would see that the action would be seen as selfish. The same field of action would be present if a person frequently repeats, "I hate people". This particular thought does not allow anyone to enter the field except the speaker. This last particular thought is very common among addicts who will do everything to please themselves even at the expense of their family and even their children.

A thought that is very common would be, "I love my family". This thought is repeated by the majority of people in the world, but it excludes people outside the family. Jesus Christ speaks in direct contrast to this thought when he answered a question about his blood brothers. His answer was, "Who is my brother and who is my sister?" I hope that you can see that His answer serves to emphasize that the thought, "Love one another" does not contain exceptions. I am not recommending one thought over another, but I am here to warn you that the thought you choose to repeat will be affecting your reality. I am also teaching you that the bigger the field of one thought such as, "Love one another", the bigger the benefit it seems to produce if the thought is positive as in the case of love. Remember that if the thought is positive, the consequence or effect will be a positive reality, but by the same token, if the thought is negative, the bigger the field of action the more negative consequences you would suffer.

When I became aware of the size of the field of action covered by the thought, "Love one another", I began to question some of my previous thinking that I had been repeating since I was a child. I have moved toward repeating thoughts of fatherly/brotherly love without exceptions. I cannot claim that I have conquered the love for humans as Christ teaches, but I continue to make progress because now I intentionally repeat that particular thought.

Imagine that all your family is murdered by an individual and he is caught in the act. Video proof is available and this individual confesses to committing the killing. There is absolutely no doubt of his guilt. My first reaction is due to the thought, "I love my family" and it excludes killers. My emotions would be one of anger and desire for his death. Indeed, most of us would express the thought , "I will never forgive him". Considering this is such a common thought about ignoring forgiveness, you would find many people who agree with your opinion.

Every time you ask a question, it becomes the point of origin to many thoughts and depending on the answer, your thought determines the direction that your brain will move. If one were to ask the question, "Should I forgive the killer?" Whatever answer you give will affect your reality. You choose your reality by the choice of thoughts you choose to repeat. When I was searching for answers in the Bible, it teaches to forgive every time without exceptions. Again, I am not trying to convince you as to what thought to believe or not, but rather I want to teach you that the Bible teaches forgiveness without exception. This means that the field of action of a particular thought is huge and thus, the benefit to forgiveness without limits creates a reality that is positive and huge.

Incidentally, I recently became aware of an old wealthy man who died in a nursing home. He never had visitors. His wealth was left to an animal shelter. It was not left to his children because he stayed angry at something that had happened in the past. His inability to forgive had caused him negative consequences and his reality was filled with loneliness. Good or bad? You be the judge, but be aware that all thoughts that you repeat become your reality. You are the master of your thoughts and therefore, creator of your reality.

I must admit that I was becoming more and more convinced that the teachings in the Bible were definitely more positive than the thoughts I grew up with. I had, just as most of you had, a mixture of thoughts many of them of uncertain origin because they were in direct contrast with what I was reading in the Bible.

One of the thoughts I have personal knowledge with was the thought, "I am fat". I remember at age 25 and in medical school thinking I was fat when I weighed only 134 pounds. Twenty years later after repeating that particular thought, it bore consequences. I was miserable reaching nearly 240 pounds without hope in sight. I began to experiment with thought by the repetition of the opposite thought, "I look great". After achieving success, I lost nearly 100 lbs. Due to the fact that I was comparing my thoughts to what the Bible was teaching, I decided to confirm that one. One verse that I came across was Psalm 139:14. Depending on the version and translation you use, you will find something similar to my transliteration, "I praise you because I look perfect and I know it". When you compare the thought, "I look great" and the thought, "I look perfect", the latter one has a bigger field of action because it removes all possibilities to any blemishes or imperfections. Since this is a positive thought and it has a bigger field, the benefit is greater when repeated over a period of time creating a more perfect reality. Of course, the logical consequence occurred when I replace my thinking with the thinking that the Bible was teaching.

I came across an interesting verse that made me change my thinking even more. I found 1 Corinthians 1:24. In that verse, Paul is trying to explain the magnitude of the gift named Christ. It reads that, "Christ is the power of God and the wisdom of God". He continued to teach about how foolish human thinking is. I decided to take this bit of information and re-write it into another verse that most Christians know, yet they do not repeat. It is found in Philippians 4:13. It states, "I can do ALL things with Christ who gives me strength". I must say that the image that it evokes gives me the ability to do things without limit because of my connection to Christ. The idea that the brain develops is like a teammate who helps when you need it the most. Since I do not repeat that thought frequently, I am left to deal with life's problems on my own with occasional assistance, almost magical by God, thus making God's presence intermittent. However, when I continually repeat Philippians 4:13, the presence and assistance of God in my daily life is constant. The difference is explained by the number of times I repeat the thought or rather my persistence in repeating this particular thought. Do keep in mind that the goal of this book is to teach you to think and therefore, any theological differences between you and me are assumed to be forgiven from the start.

I decided to see what would happen by rewriting the verse to make it easier to understand. I wrote, " I can do all things because I have the power of God and the wisdom of God". My brain could wrap around this concept much easier. Once I accepted that God was willing to give/share His wisdom and His power with me, it made it easier to repeat. Repetition of this new thought gave birth to a motivation to eliminate self imposed limits in my life. This was definitely a new concept when compared to the thoughts with which I had grown up. Most of us, during our growing years, are inspired to slay the monsters out of fear or worry. Some of us are more successful than others depending on how many monsters we feel we can kill. By the intense repetition of the particular thought that I have the power of God, my ability to destroy monsters has no end. I have become a fearless conqueror regardless of the situation. My reality is one of peace of mind because I have the knowledge that regardless of any situation I could ever encounter, I am prepared: no exceptions.

One extreme case in this area of thinking is what I find dealing with addicted behaviors. The average addict usually repeats thoughts such as, "There is nothing I can do" or "There is no hope for me". After repetition, either of these thoughts will lead to inaction. An addict enters a cycle of destruction surrounded by hopelessness that he/she would not be able to overcome. When you think in terms of the field of action, what can he/she do? The answer would be nothing or zero because the thought has become their reality.

Most of us function somewhere between, "There is nothing I can do" and "I can do all things". Most of us think that there are some things we can do and there are other things we cannot do. That is the position taken when repeating the serenity prayer. When you think in terms of the field of action, what can one do, the serenity prayer places limits on the answer. Even though the serenity prayers allows more action than the addict was previously able to do when he/she repeated, "There is nothing I can do".

Once again, this book is about training one to think correctly. Therefore, here are the thoughts one should choose. If the thought is positive, choose the thoughts with the biggest field possible such as, "I can do all things....", but when the thought is negative, choose the thought with the smallest field of action. I came to the conclusion that the thoughts I had analyzed from the Bible were big field, positive thoughts and therefore, I began changing my thinking in that direction. I recommend you do the same.

CHAPTER THIRTEEN

A CREATOR

Once when I was lecturing to a group of addicted people about thinking, I realized that one of the most difficult things for them as a group to accept is the existence of God, the Creator. Indeed, one of the first steps in recovery is the acceptance of a higher power that is bigger than any problem. When I lecture, I encourage the participants to ask questions until they understand the process of creation, the Creative Force. By now, you should be able to recite the steps easily: **Thought, Repetition, Action,** and **Outcome**. The neat thing about this energy is its ability to materialize itself into our reality. On one occasion, one of the addicts decided to ask me, as a medical doctor, if I believed that we humans were created or we just evolved as the theory of evolution explains.

My immediate answer was, "We are created" and his response was, "Prove it". I remember looking around the room and fixing my eyes on a young teenage girl. I said, "Look at her". The person asking the question looked at her. My answer was, "She was created by the Creative Force". I continued, "When her dad looked at her mother and said to himself in a thought, she looks good", and the rest was history. I turned to the person asking the question and said, "Do you think, she (the young addict) began as a thought"? His answer was, "Yes, she did in her father's mind".

It is inevitable that when people think about their own recent origins, they realize that we were all created by thought even if the thought is, "Nothing is going to happen". This is not the end of the story. As a matter of fact, it is the opposite. It is the beginning. If we were to go back in time, generation before generation, and trace back to the original man and the original woman, they both shared a thought. That thought led to procreation.

The Bible tells us that we were created by God and even among Christians there are further divisions due to different interpretations or positions we take. Other people might have a different opinion but this difference is very insignificant to our daily lives. The only thing that matters to our daily life are the thoughts we are repeating because they determine the reality we are going to experience. Lots of divisions occur because we take different opinions in the matter. As a physician, I happen to enjoy both views and to see the arguments that either side makes and simply enjoy them because neither camp seems to be able to convince the other. I assume that in 2000 years, there will be people arguing about it to no avail.

If you belong to the camp of evolution and you believe that we came from monkeys, you would agree that the Creative Force would require a thinker for the creation of the monkeys. If you want to step backward and believe that some force pressed upon something that had already existed and made it become life, you must ask, what was that force? The force that caused some atoms and molecules into a living unicellular form, followed by multicellular forms, then to fish and amphibians, then reptiles and birds, then mammals, and then humans. I know that force or a form of energy was required for all the changes that were required to take place. What was that force? Most likely, those who believe in evolution do not know and very likely will never know, yet they will want me to accept it as a fact when they themselves find no explanation. I have absolutely no trouble in believing that a force originated all the steps taken and I call the source of this force, the Creator.

Let us assume, for discussion sake, that we move back in time to the nanosecond before the Big Bang. We stop time and ask, "What was there to bang before the bang"? What caused it to bang? Again, the evolutionists would answer, "I do not know", but the Creative Force would predict the presence of a thinker who by repetition made it possible for something to go "Bang". The Creative Force cannot explain what "Banged", but if you assume that something went "Bang", there was a thinker repeating some thoughts to create what ever went "Bang" at that instant.

This book is not about creation versus evolution: this is a book about thinking. Since the beginning of my experimentation with thought, one thing became clear; the need for a thinker to produce the force. Regardless of a belief in creation or evolution, a force had to be generated in order to create the change. While those who believe in evolution failed to describe the force created, the Bible instead reports that God spoke. This little, seemingly insignificant fact becomes enormous when you realize that upon accepting the Christ, the power of God and the wisdom of God, we receive the same power to create by speaking. Even though I teach that I, the creator, must repeat the thought and that my brain is only tuned to my voice, I have to admit that both a mute person and a deaf person have the power to create. In reference to the spoken word, it only represents a form of the unit of the Creative Force, the thought itself.

In my thought exercising, I attempted to speak without thinking and I failed every time. The opposite is true that I can have thoughts without speaking or acting on them at that moment. I do have to warn you that even if you do not speak the thought, its energy appears to accumulate and cause whatever effect or action that would fulfill your particular thought. In our human case, it would appear logical that human thinking requires a connection between brain and heart. It would logically appear that when we speak, we are using the Creative Force; we are repeating a thought that is already in our heads. By speaking, we are generating the Creative Force, thus the word becomes the tool of creation.

In studying the Bible, we have found a huge number of references to a Creator who has the power to create just by speaking, much like I had discovered we have. Through repetition, we are creators in our own right. By no means equal in power to God, but having similar, yet weaker ability. This point is not difficult to see in our lives because whether you believe in God or not, we have been creating good things and bad things with our thoughts and words followed by our actions. We are the authors, creators of our own reality because no one is forcing us to repeat a particular thought. We, instead, have free choice to repeat the thoughts we choose to repeat. Until very recently, you might have not been aware that your negative thinking gave consequences and that your positive thinking was doing the same. Now, you, the thinker, know to be aware.

I would like to add a final thought to this chapter devoted to the Creator. There are occasions when we want to encourage someone. Many of us, whether believers of the Bible and God or not, refer to the thought, "With God all things are possible". This verse is intended to inspire the listener to realize that there has to exist a solution to an seemingly impossible problem. Since this beautiful thought is not repeated or believed, the listener takes on an attitude of, "God will work it out". Often one hears: "It is in God's hands".

I want to clarify this thought because it is really misunderstood. Until you begin to think about it from the point of view of the Creative Force, this particular thought does not say, "For God all things are possible" as the attitude taken by many. This verse clearly says WITH. It commands a participation in the process between the God Creator and the human creator. It is not an independent effort by God and it is not an independent process for the human creator. The repetition of this particular verse does open the mind to endless possibilities, not yet seen or imagined. I found this connection, or at least a description of the cooperation that is required for this thought to become reality. In Proverbs 16:9, it is revealed that you, the human creator, determines the goal (initial thought or direction) and that God reveals the necessary steps to achieve that goal.

In the past, I taught that when repeating a thought, the thought itself would provide you with steps required to fulfill the thought. I think that either version is correct; whether the thought reveals the steps or God reveals the steps. I have been asked during my lecturing, "Which is true, is God thought or is thought God?" The final answer is neither. While I have the ability to create good thoughts and bad thoughts, God seems to be the only source of perfect thoughts, exclusively. Finally, what then are perfect thoughts? A perfect thought is a positive thought with a huge field of action that has eternal timing. I keep finding examples of them, over and over, in the Bible.

CHAPTER FOURTEEN

WHAT DOES THE BIBLE TELL ME

My interest in the teachings found in the Bible was increasing because I was becoming more aware of the quality of the thoughts or lessons included there. I decided to dig a bit deeper to see what I could learn and what I could use in order to further my teachings of the Creative Force. The Creative Force requires the presence of a Creator or Thinker, therefore, it is not hard for me to accept the word of God. If you have grown up with a scientific background and if you believe in the Big Bang theory, you must also admit that right before the Big Bang, there was "Something" that went bang. The force that caused the change from its pre-bang state to the present state was an explosion. The "Big Bang" thinkers must accept the presence of something before the bang and also the existence of a force creating that change. What words you use to describe that "something" are very insignificant. I made peace with both sides when I began to use the word Creator or Source. You can use any of the names that are found in the Bible. It is not immediately clear why God describes himself as the Great I Am. More research needs to be done.

The bigger book, as the Bible is called in AA, begins with a description of how the Creator created everything. He spoke indicating how it was done rather than what was done. I find it amusing that the order of the creation parallels the evolutionists' and the creationists' description. Next, the Creator proceeded to create man and woman for his own pleasure. In this narration, the Bible describes those two events as separate ones. When relating to our future, the evolution camp and creation camp seem to be locked into one final outcome. The final outcome for the creation camp is the total destruction of the physical earth. That prediction is very similar to what the evolution camp speculates is going to happen to our ever changing planet.

The next part of the story occurs in the Garden of Eden where there were two trees. The tree of life and the tree of knowledge. We ate from the tree of knowledge beginning the fight between wisdom from

God and knowledge from men. This created a separation between man's thinking and God's thinking. When we rely on knowledge, we become proud and suffer its consequences while God desires us to rely on wisdom; His wisdom.

A very important question to ponder, at this point, is the fact that knowledge seems to help us deal with this green earth while God's wisdom points to something beyond this world. As humans began to populate the earth, it appears that the knowledge of man was not enough to keep us out of trouble. In order to help us, God placed leaders from time to time; from kings, to judges, to prophets. He even gave us laws to help us understand the limitations of knowledge. I have to admit that some of the books in the Bible are really confusing at first, but the stories do point out what the Creator intended from the very beginning. One example was Abraham whose faith gave him his reward. Other examples are available, but they are too numerous to mention in this book.

The law of God was written to help humans understand the problems with knowledge. In the mean time, God continues to point out the power of thinking and what thoughts to repeat. As an example in the book of Joel, we find that God wants the weak to say, "I am strong". The Creative Force was described in Joshua 1:8 and in the first Psalm. I assume that I would find more and more references if I were to search deeper.

In the Old Testament, God continually instructs man to trust Him. Indeed, the description of our future is very clear. His plan for us is to keep us safe from harm and to make us prosperous. One of the points that I find quite powerful is the simple fact that God does not give up His relationship to mankind, in spite of our treatment of Him. It becomes clear that humans, under the law, are all incapable of pleasing God 100% of the time.

After our failure to live a perfect life became obvious, the need for salvation and a savior becomes important. Mankind begins to request a savior. Those of us that use knowledge, therefore, bound to Earth, would expect a savior in human terms. A powerful general capable of destroying big armies. God's response is not to satisfy knowledge, but rather to restore the initial relationship. He makes the covenant of grace. We are to receive grace for our offenses, if we accept the wisdom of God and the power of God, also known as the Christ. The story had to be related to humans in human terms as to be understood. Instead of a powerful general, the savior is a humble, meek servant exactly opposite to what knowledge would offer. Again, the point of Christ is to offer a glimpse to something beyond this earth, such as the kingdom of God and heaven. These things cannot be accomplished by the use of knowledge, but they are easily obtained by the use of Godly wisdom. It is important to understand that the Creative Force can be used to obtain wisdom or to obtain knowledge. You are the decision maker.

The New Testament makes it clear that the law of God becomes fulfilled and therefore, it is not necessary any longer to search for a new covenant. We enter a covenant of grace. The general themes of the Old Testament are continued in the New Testament. In the New Testament, descriptions are given of the consequences of leading a life without concerning ourselves with God. The New Testament also describes the benefits of following God. It emphasizes the need to forget the past and look forward to a secure future.

One point that I like to make emphasizes the temptations of Christ before beginning his public ministry. In one particular instance, it is said that the devil, Satan, offers Jesus Christ three temptations. The desire for fame and power; for wealth and possessions; and for simple human pleasures, such as food and comfort. These things are the ones that man would obtain in this world by human effort and knowledge. Those temptations of Christ are not different than the temptations that we humans suffer while on Earth. We are especially vulnerable to those, if we are not connected to God. The Bible also emphasizes that it is best to seek the things of God; faith, wisdom, and love, the most important one being love. Of personal interest, I find that the instructions for living given to us from God are limited to human relationships and do not include the environment or lower animals. It is safe to assume that those instructions for the care and attention to animals and the environment are the result of human knowledge.

The Bible advances the idea of a kingdom, the kingdom of God, that appears to be parallel to the earthly kingdom. The Bible urges us to seek His kingdom and promises that we would receive it. Since this kingdom is not of the earth, one must seek with our heart, the origin of our thinking. This kingdom of God is obtained by grace, therefore eliminating the presumption of the need for human effort or status. It is a free gift to us, but it was not free. It was paid by God himself.

Upon accepting this gift, we are considered children of God: we are born again. The Bible teaches that this is done by the renewing of our mind, by controlling our thinking by taking every thought and changing it to fit what God has instructed us to think.

In addition to the kingdom of God, the Bible offers to the reader a final destination where there is a reunion with the Creator. The term heaven is used to describe the place where the reunion takes place. The Bible also warns us that the direction of travel of one's mind would be considered lost if we are not moving in the direction of God. This is not to say that you would suffer if you studied it from the human point of view. It is possible to have a reasonably, successful human existence with the difference of never reaching heaven since you are not connected to God. The only way to connect to the God of the Bible is by the acceptance of Jesus Christ. The reader, the thinker, must make that choice of thought and repeat it in order for it to become his/her reality.

Before I close this chapter, I need to clarify that the intent of this chapter and this book is not to convert you to my thinking, but rather to show my walk during my discovery of thinking. I am not a Bible scholar, yet I feel comfortable enough to be able, with certainty, to repeat and communicate what I have read in this wonderful source of thinking.

CHAPTER FIFTEEN

SINNER VERSUS SAINT

This is a good place to remind everybody of the work that needs to be done. Go back and re-read chapter one and make sure that you continue to do all that is required of you. Otherwise, you might not feel the energy generated by the Creative Force. In failing to do the work and only reading this book, you would have only acquired knowledge and knowledge is worthless to change your behaviors and thus your reality. You must use the Creative Force in order to change your reality. The Creative Force begins and is maintained by the repetition of specific thoughts.

As I continued experimenting with thoughts, I came upon one that bothered me considerably, "I am a sinner". This was true because it is the one I had personally repeated for many years. Remember, the creative process that generates the Creative Force: **thought** (image in head), **repetition** (words), **action** (your choices), and **outcome** (reality). I decided to put it to the test. What happens if I continue to repeat, "I am a sinner". It quickly became clear that repeating this thought generated a whole bunch of ideas, most of them clearly not good. My brain presented some choices to make and as the CARDENAS LAW predicted, I felt the attraction to do the things that were not good. The choices to which I was attracted made me feel physically good, but they were temporary pleasures. If we assume that I followed these things, which by the way I have done in the past, they left me with an empty feeling instead of the promised pleasure. One could call those actions SINS, if we are using God as the reference point. The end point was a craving for more. I experienced no satisfaction. The best way to describe it is, I became a sinner. Sinner is an attitude of "I don't care". I guess another adjective that I could use would be selfish. Definitely, it is not a wholesome picture. The consequence of repeating, "I am a sinner" was the development of an even more selfish attitude to the point of exclusion of anybody not serving my purpose. The Bible refers to this state as death and it was a spiritual death.

This thought, "I am a sinner" is very similar to, "I am worthless" or "There is something wrong with me" that I hear from my patients addicted to drugs. The final consequence of the addicts' thoughts, after walking through a very real hell here on earth, is the physical death due to overdose or illness created by the repetition of their faulty thinking.

My next step in working with this thought was to go to the point of origin. The question that needs to be correctly answered is, "Who am I?". You can have as many answers as you wish. You could answer, "I am a sinner", "I am a saint", "I am ok", "I am human", etc, etc. I chose to go to the Bible; study what the Bible said about it and how it would help me understand my true nature.

I was very familiar with some of the stories in the Bible especially from my childhood. One of the statements that bothered me since I was a little kid was the statement by God when warning Adam and Eve that if they ate from the Tree of Knowledge, "They would surely die". The same outcome occurred as when one repeats, "I am a sinner". This is a very powerful point because it makes the teachings or thoughts of the Bible very consistent from beginning to end. As a side comment, this makes the Bible more powerful because that book was written over a period of thousands of years ago, yet it remains consistent in the stories it tells and in the practical consequences of its teachings.

I was aware of the verse, Romans 3:23 that says that we all (NO exceptions) have sinned and fallen short of the standard set by God. Up to this point for me, there was a problem and no solution to the thought, "I am a sinner". I was aware of John 3:16 that says that anyone who believes in Christ should not perish but have eternal life. Again, I was attracted to the words "Death" and "Eternal life". Personally, I thought this was a neat solution to an unsurmountable problem with which I was having to deal. For many years, I had the image of a man called Jesus Christ. I was taught by many that He died because I was not a good boy. I guess they thought that this particular sacrifice was supposed to make me feel better, but it did not. It made me feel worse because now adding to the thought, "I am a sinner", I began to repeat, "I am guilty that He had to die". The outcome was an uneasy feeling of insecurity and not knowing right from wrong. Literally, I went from being somewhat confident to no confidence at all. Guilt was the term that described my state of mind. I knew that not only because of my behavior that I was a sinner, but also I added to it the fact that Christ had to die for my sin. This only added to the guilty feeling I grew up with. My way of dealing with my guilt was to avoid anything related to God because my guilt caused me to dwell on my imperfections.

Later on, as an adult who felt very intelligent, I went to a church where the power of sin was taught more than the power of grace. This led my mind to think of my inevitable trip to hell. A very similar situation I found myself was when I, the fat doctor, had to tell my patients to lose weight. This appeared to be a rather hopeless situation. I assume I felt much like those addicted to drugs.

Later on as I was reading the Bible and working on thoughts, I came across probably the neatest thought ever written, yet very obscure to the average person such as myself. In the first book to the Corinthians, Paul explained the meaning of Christ. He taught that, "Christ is the power of God and the wisdom of God". I then saw the light. Walk with me through this process so I do not lose you. Initially in the Garden of Eden, we were not sinners, but we ate from the tree of knowledge. Knowing right from wrong did not prevent us from becoming sinners without hope. In order to solve this problem, the Creator initially gave us the law and then He gave us Christ (His power and His wisdom) in exchange for me. Mankind was the cause of the problem. Upon accepting Christ, if I (or any person) use His wisdom and His power, I can receive eternal life, a clearly different outcome. You must agree that it sounds very tempting, but my mind was set on thinking. Instead of accepting it as black and white, I decided to test it.

All my Bible teachers told me that the acceptance of God's wisdom and God's power (Christ) makes you a new creation; different from the old creation. Born again is the expression most commonly used. Considering this, I went back to the Bible to see what I should call myself if I accepted Christ. Should I call myself a sinner or something else? I found multiple references in the New Testament referring to the new believers as saints. Paul writes, "To the saints of Rome". Since the term saint is opposite to sinner, I decided to test it using the creative process. What would happen if I were to begin to repeat the thought, "I am a saint" instead of "I am a sinner". From the start, I realized I could say that the new thought will create a new outcome. If you begin to repeat the thought, "I am a saint because I accepted the wisdom of God and the power of God", the initial image created in your brain is clearly different from the image of a sinner. If you continue to repeat this thought, the energy created is going to be a positive energy allowing you to make wiser, kinder, and better choices creating a neater and better outcome.

Remember that Christ means the power of God and wisdom of God. I did so when I began to repeat that thought. I felt a sense of confidence as I had never felt before. I felt emboldened to teach the creative process and to speak of the Creative Force. I continued to study the thoughts I found in the Bible and marvel and wonder about who else could have put this book together so perfectly. From beginning to end, it seems consistent as it tells the human story so clearly. It was almost as if it was written for me and my walk. It is my personal story and my struggle. It is my path and it clearly marks my destination. I felt purpose in teaching the Creative Force, therefore teaching my addicted friends became a joy, a pleasure; rather than work and difficulty.

As a general rule, all addicted people know of God, but they have their own ideas of God, not much different than most of us. We all develop thoughts of who God is. I found that changing some of those thoughts is difficult for some people. Most addicted people have been functioning using their own thinking with horrible results. The second step of the 12 step program, is to accept the existence of a caring power referred to as Higher Power or HP. I found that many of the addicted people are actually offended by the word God. Since my job is rather simple, I am compelled to teach them that their thoughts have power and that the repetition of those thoughts have caused their consequences. The solution is rather fast and easy. All they have to do is stop using their own thoughts and begin using the thoughts that their HP gives them. Personally, I do not get bothered by the fact that they do not claim to be Christians. I simply teach them that their thoughts have consequences and that appears to be what God wants me to continue to do. As I come to understand the thoughts of addicted people, it becomes obvious to me that God has challenged me to prepare their minds to learn the good news as only the Bible lessons can teach.

On many occasions when I use the example of sinner versus saint, some of my addicted friends walk out of the meeting because they find the idea of calling themselves saints too offensive. This brings me to an important set of thoughts that we all seem to possess and that are affecting each of us on a daily basis. Depending on how you answer the questions that originate your thoughts, God becomes a different image in your head.

Personally, I call God the Creator or my Source. Again, I do not think that the word that you use makes as big of a difference as the image that you develop in your head. Some of the questions to ponder are: Is God in control all the time? Is God a mean, demanding dictator? Is God a loving, caring father? Is God going to provide your needs, your wants, or the desires of your heart? Does God answer all your prayers or does He pick and choose? Can I trust God to deliver all of His promises?

At this point In my personal walk, I was beginning to understand the Bible teachings at a very deep level, but in all honesty, there were big holes in my understanding. When one looks at human suffering, one cannot help but wonder how a loving, caring God allows suffering to occur? Why do children die? Was God aware of their deaths? If God was aware, did He choose not to do anything about those? Why are there two million children aborted every year in the USA? Why are there six million world-wide deaths every year due to starvation? How we choose to answer those questions is going to create an image of God in our heads and the repetition of that image (a thought) is going to give consequences. The image gives you the choices from which to choose. As a brief example, if I choose to see God as a dictator, most likely I am going to act as a dictator as I relate to other humans, but if I see God as a caring, loving being, my actions will be a reflection of that image in my brain. Therefore, my actions would be that of a caring and loving person; just as the image of my Creator appeared in my head.

CHAPTER SIXTEEN

THE GODS WE MAKE AND THE GOD OF THE BIBLE

The addicts that I have come to know and love frequently repeat a thought that is very destructive; "I will always need drugs". Thankfully by the time I enter the picture, they are already in treatment. According to the Creative Force if you think and repeat that thought for a long period of time, you will create a strong desire to use drugs even to the point that this drive to use will have no limits. The end result is a constant dependency on the drugs.

If you look at the resulting behavior, the CARDENAS LAW predicts that the addict will lie, cheat, steal, cause physical harm, and destroy all with only one purpose: to obtain drugs. Indeed if taken to the extreme, the addict is willing to kill or to die for the sole purpose of obtaining the chosen drug. The choice of losing a home, a spouse, children or the chosen drug to get high is a rather easy one for the addict. Nothing else will fulfill the thought, "I will always need drugs".

What we, the outsiders, observe is an irrational drive to do the things that we know are not good. The driving force or the force causing these actions is the Creative Force caused by the repetition of the faulty thought or thoughts in the mind of the addict. It is not surprising to find that the addict uses drugs with the full knowledge that what they are doing is destructive. They do not know that the driving force has been created in their own minds by their mere repetition of their poor thoughts. The drug has become their god. They breathe, work, and function by the drug's gospel. The ultimate price to pay to that god is their possessions, health, family, children, and eventually their life.

Often times, I have wished that the cause of addiction was a single thought such as, "When I grow up I want to be an addict". Changing that one thought could cure all the addicts easily. All of us, however, live in realities. All of our realities are created by all our thoughts coming together at the same time and at the same place affecting what we feel and see. As the consequence of all of us having different thoughts, our realities cannot be identical, but portions of our realities can be similar.

Therefore, we can experience certain portions of reality together.

The description that I used to describe the behavior of addicts is very similar (same process) to certain negative thoughts that the untrained mind would have the tendency to repeat. It is my sincere goal that you would be able to recognize that since you have thoughts, you could become trained on their use. Using the Creative Force to your personal benefit will enable you to help those around you.

A friend of mine was dumped by his girlfriend and this poor fellow was having a bad time dealing with that. He was unable to get up, go to work, take a shower, and just simply function. His mother asked me to help him. By that time, I was an expert on the mirror exercise and was bold about teaching people the consequences of their thinking. I felt prepared. I found him watching television with the sound muted and looking into the air, lost in his own world. My first question was beautiful, "What are you thinking?".

His answer said it all, "She is my life". Tears began to flow from his eyes. I quickly asked him to say, "I hate her". His look was almost like I was Satan. I asked him to repeat it, and repeat it, and repeat it. You get the point. After several repetitions, his smile broke through. Then without prompting, he began to repeat it, "I hate her". The energy of the Creative Force was beginning to break the old thought, "She is my life". I began to explain to him the consequence of our thinking. Eventually, I left him with homework much like the work I recommended in the first chapter of this book; the work that needs to be done. I left him to write daily, "I will be fine". I have spoken to his mother on occasion and she reports that he has become a different man. He is confident that he is able to deal with anything that life throws at him and is constantly repeating, "I will always be fine".

I hope you begin to see that the poor fellow in the story had created a god, the girlfriend. Before his thinking changed, his happiness was determined by his god, his girlfriend. When people repeat the thought he did or as many men say, "If mama ain't happy, nobody is happy", disastrous outcomes occur. When you begin to analyze the thought, "She is my life" and repeats this thought, that thought becomes your reality. That thought has a huge field; all things are ordered, organized, and selected by that thought. Such thoughts will tell you what to eat, when to eat, what to wear, and even what to think. This fellow may have been able to function for a little while, but upon abandonment, his life would have appeared impossible, thus making him unable to function. I suspect you would describe this person as needy. Spineless is the term I prefer to use. He did not have thoughts of his own, He only repeated the thought given to him by her. In her defense, I have to say that in the beginning of their relationship, the girl may have found that trait attractive, but very quickly it became a very, heavy load to bear, thus the dumping.

By asking him to repeat the thought, "I hate her", I was attempting to break the bondage created in his mind by his own thinking. Freedom came after repeating, "I will be fine". This particular thought creates a door, a walkway, leading to a place of safety and comfort created by oneself in one's own mind, irrespective of the circumstances at the present time.

The previous two examples were presented to demonstrate that we humans frequently create our gods in our minds all the time. The question that comes to mind then is, "How do you know you are following the correct God?" That was my hesitation to change from the God of my childhood to the God of my adulthood. I had to start thinking about the thoughts I was having about God. Empowered by the creative process, I began to use the Creative Force to help me clean my brain of the negative aspects with which I had grown up; and to make certain I was replacing them with positive thoughts. I was going to use the Bible as a guide since I was developing a stronger attraction for it. I was finding that the Bible contained many positive thoughts with large fields of action, but there were still lingering questions in my mind.

One of the thoughts I had grown up with was the idea that God was watching me and He was going to strike at any moment when He got fed up with me. After 57 years of willful disobedience, God has not done that. Therefore, my thought of a God ready to strike me, at the least of my mistakes, appears to be wrong. The description of God in the Bible suggests exactly the opposite. It suggests a patient, caring, loving God willing to die for me and willing to give me the privilege of calling myself a child of God. This switch in thinking, imagining God as a human father, did not appear to be a difficult decision for me because as a father the negative actions of my own children were never enough to cause me to stop loving them.

One of the aspects of God that became clear to me when reading the Bible is the fact that the God of the Bible requires a relationship, a cooperation between God and me. I had grown up with the idea that God was distant and He wanted it that way. His will for my life would not change. The picture of my reality was beginning to become more clear. There are many people in the world who are not connected to God; they have the simple knowledge that there is a God, but in their daily thinking, they continue to function without any regard to His wisdom or His power. One such example occurs when certain tragic things happen such as a flood, a hurricane, or a car accident. At those moments, millions of people call on the God of the Bible and since there was no previous connection, the communication appears unanswered. Going back to the very beginning of time when we lost the connection to God by eating from the Tree of Knowledge, God did not give up the relationship. God attempted to communicate to us through prophets, judges, and kings, but to no avail. We, the human race, kept on ignoring his requests. The most striking thing I learned from studying multiple passages is that the God of the Bible is persistent, but He appears to have a time limitation. At some point, the God of the Bible will let the people suffer the consequences of their own human thinking.

This brings us to a very important question that has not been answered with enough energy for me to accept. Why is it that bad things happen to some apparently, good people? I know there is a book with that title. Remember, that I am coming from the point of view of the creative process and the Creative Force. Remember, that the Creative Force teaches that any thought I repeat is going to become my reality. Therefore when bad things happen to godly people, my first question would be, "Was this created by humans or God?". Several examples come to my mind.

Imagine the pastor who has an affair; a very common problem in our society. Let us first see the affair as the outcome of a process of creation that began with the pastor's thinking. It is easy to predict that the first thought that occurred in the pastor's mind would have been something such as, "She looks hot", referring to a woman other than his wife. Again, the process of creation teaches me that the pastor must have repeated the thought that led to some actions such as; lying to his wife, sneaking around his schedule, and eventually having sex with a woman other than his wife. In this scenario, the God of the Bible allows the pastor to travel the road of his own destruction. Therefore, the God of the Bible does not force you to think any specific thought. It appears that is where man's free will rests. I choose the thoughts I repeat. This particular observation definitely made me change the idea of my childhood. My image of God changed from that of a dictator, police God into a more mature idea of God who grants me the freedom to choose the thoughts I repeat.

In this circumstance of when bad things happen to good people, I could blame God or I can blame man, the pastor. The actions of a pastor having an affair are not caused by God, but rather by the individual allowing the repetition of some human negative thinking to occur. The Bible teaches that we are to exercise control over our thoughts as described in the second book written by Paul to the Corinthian church. You will find this description in chapter 10, verse 5. I have decided that the God of the Bible demands a relationship with me and requires that I repeat the thoughts of God. It warns me not to use my own thinking. Again, that description is found in James 1:13. After reading those two verses, I must admit I was liking my adult version of the God of the Bible more and more.

I wish to conclude this chapter with the realization that all of us have several thoughts about God that we have learned during our lifetime depending on the experiences we have had. As time passes, we are likely to modify our thoughts and we may or may not choose to repeat them. It is the repetition of the thoughts that we choose that reveals aspects of God and they become our truth. It is not that God changes, but rather that our ability to see aspects of God depends on our thinking. At this point, it was becoming more obvious to me that when comparing my thinking of God to the God described in the Bible that I had been praying to the wrong god. A god of my own making.

The Creative Force has its practical purpose to show you in your mind what the thoughts you are repeating are going to do. If I repeat, "God is my absolute provider, my source of everything", I am going to start to believe that the good things and the bad things in my life are from God. My brain will not show me what I am doing wrong that caused the bad things in my life. I found in the book of James that the God of the Bible is the source of only the perfect gifts in my life. I needed to modify my thinking to, "God is my provider of the good things in my life" which is more consistent with what the Bible has taught from the very beginning. This is repeated when we read that famous verse, Jeremiah 29:11 that describes the plans God has for my life. On the other side of the coin when bad things happened in my life (they were my outcomes), I came to realize that most of them occurred as a result of my poor thinking.

My solution to the problem was to start experimenting with the thoughts used in the Bible to describe God. It was a simple matter of repetition before I began to see a different God; a true and mighty God. Most of us have multiple thoughts to describe God and the Bible. The Bible uses multiple names to describe God. Depending on the thought we repeat, that is the aspect of God that is revealed to us. For example: if I have only a soft belief that God will protect me and make me prosperous and I add to it thoughts such as, "You never know" and "I have no luck", then the God that I would see would be a God that is not in absolute control, but a god where some things are under the control of other forces such as karma, luck, and the unknown. However, If I use the thought from the Bible only, I begin to see a different God; powerful, yet loving. One of the most reassuring verses I have found in the Bible is one when Jesus Christ is explaining to the apostles how to achieve entrance to the kingdom of Heaven. He must have been around children because He said, "You must be like one of these to enter the kingdom". What I began to do was to pay attention to the thinking of children. Their thinking is magical and without fear. It appears that as we grow up we change from that pure vision of God to one changed by the fears we all create and entertain in our minds.

CHAPTER SEVENTEEN

A BAD EXAMPLE

The creative process and the Creative Force have allowed me to see the world in a totally different way. While the average person sees the actions of another person, I immediately focus on their thinking not excusing their action, but rather explaining the origin of their action. When I teach this process in the addiction class, I encounter difficulty when I attempt to explain sin, the law of God, and the grace of God.

If you take an action, that most would consider typical, such as drinking beer in Germany, most people would see it as normal, nothing negative. Now, let us examine drinking of the same beer in Saudi Arabia. It would be important for you to know that beer in that country does not contain alcohol, but in this case and for this particular example, the beer consumed does contain alcohol. Most people in Saudi Arabia would consider the action of drinking the beer negative. It is not the action, but rather the thinking that causes an action to be deemed good or bad.

I ran into the same difficulty when explaining the covenant of the law versus the covenant of grace that is taught in the Bible. In order to relate to my audience this concept, the first example that came to my mind was not necessarily a good one given that I was teaching at the rehab center, but since it was a very effective explanation, I kept on using it. The bad example begins like this: imagine you have four ounces of marijuana in your possession while you are driving in Kentucky in the year 2017. The police stopped and had a reason to search you and they found the marijuana. Since marijuana is illegal in this state with laws that punish that particular behavior, you are charged with a violation of the law. The judge will give you consequences. Thus far, it is easy to understand that where there are laws, there are also consequences. Now let us imagine that you had moved to Colorado where there is no law against marijuana. Let us imagine the same scenario. You are stopped and searched by the police and they find four ounces of marijuana. Since there is no law against its use, there are no consequences.

Just as this difference is difficult for the average Christian in the USA to understand, it is even more difficult for an addict who has a faulty idea of the God of the Bible to appreciate. This is a frequent point of contention for the addicted people when I try to teach the Creative Force. The Bible teaches that after losing the connection to God, the law was given to us humans. The purpose of these laws was to show us that all of us, without exception, were unable to meet the standard set by God. Therefore, God enters a new covenant of grace. This covenant says that if we accept His wisdom and His power we are admitted into his kingdom where there is no law. In the past when man was under the law and if he got drunk, he would be judged guilty. Now that he is under grace and gets drunk, his action is no longer counted as sinful because where there is no law; there is no sin. It is not that his behavior is perfect, good, or bad. It is just that his behavior is simply not under judgement because after accepting Christ he began to live under grace.

I am not a trained Bible scholar and I am not advocating getting drunk. I use this example to explain to my students that the God of the Bible does not seem to worry as much about their actions as they do. The God of the Bible seems to worry more about the state of their hearts where thoughts originate. Therefore, I shout to the students, "Do not worry about your actions, worry more about your thinking". It is your thinking that determines your actions as I explained in the CARDENAS LAW.

Just to make things clear, I am not advocating getting drunk or just ignoring all bad behaviors. Paul explains that; although everything is possible, everything is not good. When it comes to your behaviors and your body, the Bible makes it very clear that we are to treat our bodies as the temple of God.

If I apply the Creative Force to the thought, "My body is the temple of God", this is a huge thought. The fields it covers would include my exercise, my sleep, my sex life, my diet, etc., thus affecting only the behaviors I choose to repeat.

Most of us have a personal difficulty accepting grace, not because grace is a difficult concept to understand, but rather because we are constantly repeating thoughts about equality; right and wrong; justice and injustice; and action and consequences. We are constantly repeating thoughts about getting even and punishment. Anytime we see something controversial on Facebook or television, we automatically judge based on the thoughts we have been repeating.

At a personal level, I began to experiment with the thoughts of grace. Again, I started beaming like a teenager who had been kissed for the first time. I realized that grace cannot be given by God or anyone else until a wrong is acknowledged. After a few repetitions of, "I grant you grace" (that was my thought), it became clear that the listener must be made aware of the negative action. When I do something wrong in the eyes of God because I am under a covenant of grace, God does not count it as a sin. However, it is the job of the Holy Spirit to point out that my behavior is outside His expectation. Otherwise, I would not know that I was given grace.

Let us use, for example, a teenager who had never been trained in the proper disposal of garbage. Every time this person walked by my neat clean lawn, he dropped his garbage not because he is evil, but rather because of the lack of training. I have two options. One: I can pick up his garbage without saying anything. I can do that for a lifetime and his behavior will never change. My action of picking up his garbage is not grace. He, most likely, would never be aware of my existence. Two: I can approach him and instruct him (give him the law). He is now aware that his action should be to avoid putting his garbage on my manicured lawn. Assuming his best intention on a day when he is distracted, the teen does place some garbage on my lawn. Now the offense has taken place and since I am playing the role of the god of my yard, I find myself with two choices. Choice one is that I can impose the law and beat him or choice two is that I can grant him grace after pointing out his offense. The second one is more difficult because it requires that I forgive the trespass. As the god of my lawn, I choose to show and grant him grace because I love the teen more than my own lawn. Who removed the garbage you asked? I did, the god of the lawn.

So it is with the God of the Bible. After losing our connection to God, He gave us laws. Our actions are now judged. We know the laws, but as most teens, we act as if the laws were not written for us. We keep on dumping garbage on God's lawn, his creation. The good news is that God granted us grace. That in spite of our actions, He chooses to love us and ignore our transgressions of the law. However, the law can not be ignored. The standard does not change. The law must be fulfilled. "How was it fulfilled?", you might ask. The answer is by God Himself in the form of Jesus Christ.

I do not know your thoughts about God, but in my personal walk, the Bible teaches something that I learned from the Creative Force that made me like the God of the Bible. I was finally learning the idea of the cross, sin, and grace. My thinking was definitely changing. At a practical level, what I was learning about God and His love for me was changing my relationship with my children. The God of the Bible did not quit trying to have a relationship with me in spite of my attitude. Instead, He paid the price to restore our relationship, thus fulfilling the law, not changing it. Once the law is fulfilled through Christ, we enter the covenant of grace for those who accept His gift. Becoming aware of the amount of love required to love me in spite of my teen attitude, gave me, as an adult, the desire to seek and serve the God of the Bible. My purpose in life was becoming clear: I am to teach my children, all seven billion of them that the God of the Bible loves them to death.

CHAPTER EIGHTEEN

ANGER, GUILT, AND DEALING WITH MY PAST

The blessings bestowed upon me continue to pour with the use of the Creative Force. This energy that is created by the repetition of thoughts has allowed me to find things that were hidden from me and from most humans. As I practiced and experimented with thinking, it became easier and easier to see how the world really functions and how to change it quickly depending on your goals. Literally, with thoughts, we are only limited by our imagination. If I make my imagination better and better, I can create a better and better world.

The creative process of **thinking, repetition, actions,** and **outcome** is eternal and we, humans, have used it and will continue to use it for the rest of our lives. Our awareness of the process or our lack of awareness of the process does not allow us to escape its consequences. After years of experience with thinking, I feel the confidence to be able to give you a clear pathway from your problem; to your solution all the time. Literally, there is nothing impossible for the human mind. In order to deal with issues such as the past, anger, guilt, and fear in my addiction classes, I feel like a duck in the water; calm, cool, and collected.

As a quick refresher course, you must remember that the energy created by the Creative Force has certain limits such as; the thought can only become itself, the energy only affects the thinker, and the number of repetitions is proportional to the size of the field and the time of the thought. If you have any problems with these concepts, all you have to do is re-read (repeat) the initial chapters and continue to do the work that must be done that is found in chapter one.

One of the most common stumbling blocks for the healing of addiction is the inability that the addicts have in dealing with their past. This also applies to the average, non-addicted person. The lack of awareness that the energy contained in thoughts causes a block to personal success. In many cases, it continues to block the thoughts vital to success. However, it is liberating to know that the power that caused ones problems can be easily manipulated. It is up-lifting to know that there is nothing wrong with an addict except the lack of training. It is reassuring that the problems are not a genetic defect, or a character defect, or an intelligence deficit. This knowledge propels one in the right direction. The recognition of this process does not free one from his/her problems because knowledge does not change behavior. Knowledge, merely, points out that one must choose the right thought and repeat it in order to move in the right direction. It is the number of repetitions that creates the energy required to change one's behaviors. It is the consequences of one's new behaviors that one must accept as one's new reality. The consequence of not accepting this simple process and its power causes one to continue to try to solve problems that have affected many people throughout the world and for many centuries in ways that have added to their problems and not their solutions. All of one's problems were created by one's thinking and therefore, all the solutions must be created starting with one's thinking. Any attempt to solve one's problems by changing behavior without changing thinking will be futile and frustrating with short lived success. To the alcoholic, it is liberating to know that alcohol has no power except for the power given to alcohol by the thinker. This also applies to any problem that is affecting anybody at this point.

A common thought that I hear is, "You cannot change the past". I admit I have repeated the same thought. If I continue to repeat that thought then the reality created would be one that would make my past impenetrable. The unchanged past would continue to harm me for the rest of my life. In experimenting with thought, I decided to repeat the opposite. I began to repeat, "I can change the past". Remember, it is just a thought. I am not asking you to do anything else, but to repeat that thought. I did. Quickly, images of all the movies referring to time travel came to mind. This is not a book about science fiction, although science fiction has the annoying tendency of becoming our reality. That is an interesting observation.

I began to see possibilities such as, "I can forget the past", "I can forgive the past", and "I can relive the past". These thoughts suggested that the past appears to be like molding paste. I could have positive actions with those, if I repeated the appropriate thought. I began to realize that my past was a set of memories; good, bad, and neutral. Those were the thoughts that I kept repeating in my brain . The thought, "I can change the past" became true because my past is only a series of thoughts and I became an expert on changing thoughts. Consequently, the thought, "You cannot change the past", which I lived with for many years, had to go. That thought was like a wall that prevented me from enjoying or replacing the thoughts that made up my past.

The recognition that my past is made up of memories, thoughts that are replayed in my head, made me jump to the easy step to classify my memories into good or bad categories. I quickly realized that I had not been repeating many of my happy memories. I began to repeat memories, such as ones similar to the on the day my 12 year-old brother kicked an eight year-old boy that was bullying me when I was only seven. That was a very proud moment for me. That memory reminded me that I was never alone. Apparently, my problems resulted when the memories I chose to repeat were the bad ones and not the good ones. The amazing part of this process is that no one forces me to repeat one thought versus the other. I am the one in control of my thinking. I decided to repeat only good memories; like my mother saving the last pieces of soap to make larger balls for our family to use. On an interesting note, I decided to speak to my brothers and sisters about the good memories we had shared. I also decided that the ball of left over soaps was such a good memory that I made some and then gave one to each of my brothers and sisters. That simple action of re-living a good memory created a magical moment; like time sitting still. The atmosphere of the room immediately changed when I presented them with my simple gift. The shared thoughts created a magical time, thus generating another good memory. Now, I am actively speaking of the good memories from the past.

My past is not only the collection of good memories, but also some bad ones. Only recently have I become aware of the consequences of remembering and repeating the bad thoughts. Now, I realize that dwelling on those details caused my present reality. I divided the negative thoughts into two general categories. Category one included the memories when I was offended, hit, or victimized. Category two included the memories of when I offended, hurt, or hit another person. The result of repeating the bad memories have huge consequences and determine who I am today. I realized the thoughts I repeat shape my future. I must learn to control my thinking.

For example, imagine that a person, as a child, was sexually abused. The child was touched in an inappropriate manner. Unfortunately, this memory is very common to many people. As a result, I intentionally choose this as an example of a bad thought. Whether the child reports the abuse or not is not very significant. What is important is how often the child repeats the memory. It is the number of repetitions that determines the power created. If the child continually repeats the abuse memory, the child's brain will only reveal the action that completes the thought. Soon, the image of a victim appears in the child's head. The actions of the child are going to be those that will lead the child to act and behave as a victim. Eventually, the thinker sees himself/herself as a victim in all circumstances because the thought eventually became the thinker's reality. What results is an angry, hurtful, distrustful, unhappy person who is likely to experience depression.

Can I or anyone change that reality? The answer is yes, but only if we can change the thought. I may not be able to change exactly what happened, but I surely can change what I think about it. One of the choices that we humans have is to forgive. It is not the only choice, but it is the choice I recommend. If I begin to repeat thoughts of forgiveness, love, and strength, those actions (the sexual abuse) will not define me. I suggest the repetition of, "I am stronger than any problem in my life". Due to the fact that I have chosen the high road, one of strength, the picture that develops in my mind would be different. My actions would be different as predicted by the CARDENAS LAW and the outcome, or my present reality, would be different.

Another example that can illustrate my point is to imagine that a parent in a moment of frustration calls his/her child a loser. Two things that the Creative Force teaches us is that the parent's thinking has no power except to put a thought in the child's mind; and the most important point is that the thinker, whoever repeats the thoughts, is the one that creates the power. In this example, the child has the power to choose to repeat the thought or ignore it. It is the child that must choose to forgive the parent or not. If the child chooses not to forgive and continues to repeat, "I am a loser" even if the parent never said it again, this child is going to create a negative energy which will cause negative choices. The reality created will be negative. Most likely, that child will grow up to be someone who is irresponsible, unemployed, poor, and with low aspiration for the future.

Now, imagine that I teach this person that his/her thinking has power. I would not try to explain the parent's actions, but I would focus on this person's thinking. Through forgiveness and changing the thought from, "I am a loser" to "I can do all things through Christ who gives me strength" or "I am a child of God", positive changes occur. This simple action of changing a thought begins the process of creation. The strength of this energy is proportional to the number of repetitions. If this individual starts repeating the new thought intentionally, either by speech or by writing, the time necessary to change his/her actions is going to be short, creating a different reality. The person is able to change his/her past because the past is made up of thoughts and by forgiving those who have hurt and offended him/her releases their anger and frustration. That person becomes a new creation.

    Regardless of the problem, one can fix any situation if one thinks of these processes in reverse. Let us begin with your anger issues. Imagine that anger is your reality. Due to the fact that your anger is caused by your actions and your actions are created by your thoughts, the simplest solution would be to change your thinking. Therefore, my warning to you is, "I want you to change your past". You must change the thoughts that caused your anger. If you choose to hold onto anger by repeating such thoughts as, "I will never forgive him/her", expect the consequences of that thought. No one is forcing you to think the thoughts that you choose to repeat. If you want your anger gone, I recommend forgiveness.

    Take a moment to remember all the horrible things you have done to God. From ignoring Him, to hating him, and to all thoughts between. His anger was resolved when he chose to forgive us. That did not happen because all of a sudden we felt the need to honor Him. The Bible teaches that when we were yet sinners, God chose to forgive. When you forgive those who have offended you, you are using the same pattern that God chose. It is God's action that reconnects us to Him. Therefore, it is your action of forgiveness that releases you from the bonds of anger in your life.

    Moving forward: my past also included the thoughts and memories when I was the offender. I realized it was important to correctly deal with those memories. The one that came quickly to my mind was the one that occurred when I was a child growing up in a small town in Colombia. There, you could easily walk one block to the grocery store. One day my father gave me the equivalent of today's 20 dollar bill to buy a pound of sugar which would actually cost about one dollar. I ran to the store and bought the sugar. By the time I came back, my father had left for work. I put the change in my coat with the full intention to give the extra money back later that day. Several days went by, I forgot the money, my father forgot the change, and I did not wear the coat again for a while. About a month later, to my surprise, I found the money. To a child my age, that was a great deal of money. The dilemma I faced was whether to give the money back or not.

No surprise: I chose to think about it a little bit longer. Little by little the money was spent. The matter was forgotten by my father, but not by me. The event remained in my mind and every time my father called my name, I imagined what was about to happen. The big catastrophe was around the corner; I was going to get a beating; many thoughts were going through my mind. My anxiety and guilt never ceased. They only got worse because I never stopped breaking rules. I began to drive without a driver's license. I drove without insurance. I cheated on my girlfriend, even though I had a good relationship with her. All the lies, thefts, cheating, and other things that I thought I was getting away with, I was not. It was as if I was carrying a heavy backpack, but what I was actually carrying were the secrets that caused my shame and guilt. Every time I met someone, it was like having a split personality. I spoke with a loud voice to the person in front of me, but the other personality spoke with a softer, inner voice to myself. Internally, I was repeating those thoughts that made up the shameful part of my past.

I encountered the question, "Can I change my past?". The answer is yes, but you and I must change our thinking. I could change the thought to, "I do not care" about what I did in the past (I do not recommend this) or I could ask for forgiveness (highly recommended). You can also follow the recommendations found in the big book of AA such as making amends. Making amends has the power to change your past and since changing your past is now possible you are not the same. You become a new you. You free yourself from the shame caused by remembering your ugly past.

After becoming a physician and carrying the guilt of keeping the $19, I decided to make amends to my father even if I could not right all the other wrongs I had committed. At least I could forgive myself for keeping the extra money. I calculated a cheap interest rate and I wrote a letter explaining the check for $500 that I was sending. I walk lighter today knowing that my father has forgiven me for a wrong that he had never noticed. I had paid a much larger price for a very long time, but now I have liberated myself from the haunting memory of the past, simply by changing my thinking.

There are places where amends are impossible. I cannot literally correct the wrong of driving without a license, but I can follow traffic laws today. I just simply accept general forgiveness. I do not beat myself up. I am a new creation because changing my past has the power to change my present reality.

All of this knowledge and insight that I began recognizing was due to the fact that I was using the Creative Force. In addition, this forced me to read and compare my thinking with what the Bible was teaching. In the Bible I found that in order to continue our relationship with God, He gave us the law: a behavior code, if you will, that defines our actions. The purpose of these laws is to prove to us humans what God already knew. Our actions, even in the best of times and with the best intentions, are not going to meet the standard required to reconnect to God. We can reconnect to God because He wants to re-establish that lost connection. He does not change the rule or law, but rather fulfills all the requirements of the law by He, Himself paying the price.

A similar situation occurs when we forgive. We simply choose to pay the price required by the offense when we are motivated by love. We could, when offended, request amends as it is required by the law, but in the latter case we get justice. If we choose to forgive like God chooses, we grant grace which is much more beneficial to us humans. The act of kindness of extending grace or receiving grace seems to have all the healing power required to lift us to a higher plane of existence where we are meant to live.

For all the times that I have ignored God in the past, the Bible teaches that I am granted grace after accepting God's gift given in the form of Christ. Jesus Christ repaid the debt required by the law. So the law is fulfilled. I am forgiven and now live under grace; reconnected to God.

Please remember, that the ability to understand these concepts written in the Bible was only possible because I began to repeat the thought, "I can change my past". This particular thought, "I can change my past" is really only a small portion of a bigger thought, "I can control time". I have to admit that until now I must have been repeating the thought, "I cannot control time" because until I discovered the Creative Force, I had felt unable to change the past and I was also fearful of my future.

CHAPTER NINETEEN

FEAR, THE WILL OF GOD, CREATING MY FUTURE

The creative process teaches me that I, the thinker, have the power to choose the thoughts I repeat. The energy generated by the repetition of a particular thought has the limitation of only affecting the field that the particular thought describes. The repetition of thoughts began very early in life. Therefore, I, the thinker, have been creating my reality little by little. When a particular thought changes, my reality is changed only to the extent described by the thought. There is an element of time that is needed between the time of thoughts change to the materialization of those thoughts.

If you were to think about your reality today, some of the thoughts have already materialized while other thoughts are in the different stages of the creative process. Some of the thoughts have started to cause actions while other thoughts have just begun the process. They may not have had enough time to create the image in your brain. The thoughts that have already materialized would be what you would call your past while the thoughts that are ending the creative process would be called your present. The thoughts that you have just begun to repeat plus the thoughts that you might repeat later would be called your future.

In the previous chapter, we took time to analyze your thoughts that formed your past. We discovered that there are some thoughts that are bad (produced bad outcomes like anger, guilt, shame) and other thoughts that were good (produced good outcomes like family, childhood memories). A similar analysis can be done for the thoughts that are going to be creating your future. It becomes imperative that we begin a process of analysis of all these thoughts, thus giving us control over our future.

Think of your future, all of your future, like a puzzle. Each piece is produced or rather will be produced by a thought that you repeat today or a thought that you will repeat starting in the future. Remember, that each thought has a particular size or field of effect. Depending on the size of these fields, the number of pieces in your puzzle will vary.

If I begin to repeat the thought, "I cannot change my destiny" and I start to repeat it day and night over a long period of time soon an image of my future will appear. My entire future would appear to be out of my control: a huge field because it describes all my future actions and experiences. The consequence of this thought is that I begin to feel that I have no control over what is going to happen and when it will occur. We generally expect bad things to happen, so the overall reality created would be one of constant anxiety and frustration because we would not be able to change our circumstances. We would be in a constant state of fear, probably needing to be medicated to be able to function in the present time. Please keep in mind that a negative thought about your future is the cause of fear and this fear created by the thinker only has one victim, the thinker.

My recommendation is not to repeat the thought, "I cannot change my destiny". Instead, I suggest the opposite thought, "I control my future". I must admit that when I began to repeat this latter thought there were some doubts in my mind. I personally did not believe it to be true, but to me it was simply an experiment. The creative process supported this statement because all I had to do was control my thinking and I would be home free. The immediate response was to create the question, "Can I control all the thoughts I repeat?". If you choose to answer, "No, I do not control all my thoughts", your future would be uncertain. However, if you choose the answer, "Yes, I can control all my thoughts", the future comes back again under your control. Remember, that up to this point of the experiment, all you need to do is the repetition of a particular thought and the observation of what happens in your brain. Easy to do.

If I start to repeat, "I do not control my thoughts", you will find yourself experiencing that the thought becomes true. You will give up control, feel the inability to do something about it, and feel the frustration that you know better, yet you are unable to change your reality. Again, the repetition of this thought would generate anxiety and fear. Personally, I began to repeat the thought, "Yes, I control my future because I control all my thoughts". The repetition began and the results started to come in.

I quickly became aware of the thoughts that I had been repeating for a long time, only to realize that most of the thoughts I had been repeating were negative. Keep in mind that the larger the number of thoughts, the larger the number of puzzle pieces that make up your future. The realization that my future was dependent on multiple thoughts made me realize the need to reduce the number of thoughts. In the past I repeated, "Karma is a witch". The consequence of that thought was that a portion of my future was dependent on a force called karma which became stronger based on the number of times that I repeated that specific thought. The elimination of that thought caused the number of puzzle pieces to become less. Other thoughts such as, "You never know" was repeated frequently and became my reality. Such thoughts had to be eliminated because the field of action was huge.

Among other thoughts that came up for analysis was, "I have no luck"; this particular one removes the possibility of something nice happening to me randomly. One of the thoughts whose outcome surprised me the most was, "I am getting old". The image generated by this thought is one of a feeble, weak, demented, incapable, dependent, sick individual. Definitely a negative image, but the awareness of its existence would have not been possible if I had not been repeating, "Yes, I control my future". Therefore, that particular thought had to go too. By this time, it was becoming clear that the simple process of eliminating thoughts was not going to be enough. It was almost like an attractive force leading to the fact that the thoughts removed had to be replaced. My image of the future included thoughts about my health, my relationships, my children, my wife, my service to the community. The task at hand began to appear complex, except for the fact that thoughts can be added. If I add all the thoughts that affect me, I would come with a big thought, "MY LIFE". Now, it was a matter of determining the direction for which I wanted to send my life.

If I choose to repeat, "Life is hard", my future would be a series of difficult experiences that most likely would make me a bitter person. Most people, in general, repeat thoughts such as, "My life is OK". This can be translated to say the sum of their good and bad experiences is tolerable, but if given the choice to remove the negative experiences they would. The removal would be an acceptable improvement. The frustration occurs in not being aware of the Creative Force. We accept our inability to shape our future. My personal experiment became easy. I began to repeat, "My life is better and better" and on occasion I would switch to, "My life is perfect". This latter thought created an image that I had seen as a child when I believed in my absolute ability. As time passed, I had begun to put up walls and close doors. All this was done to the point that the perfect image from my childhood had begun to fade. However, the repetition of the thought, "My life is perfect" was bringing back that image into sharper and sharper focus. One of the most striking bits of the image that took me by surprise was the purity of my heart. I wanted to help everyone, every where in the world, without the worries of adequate money. Indeed those were the thoughts that we, my brothers and sisters, repeated as children: "I am going to leave this world in better shape than it was when I was born".

The repetition of this thought, "My life is perfect" was creating a purpose for my life. Strangely enough, I began to realize that up until that day I was living my life just getting by, instead of the exhilarating feeling I was beginning to develop. I was acquiring a strong decisive purpose for my life.

The next step of my search was to compare the thoughts that were relevant to my future that anyone could easily find in the Bible. A flood of reference came to mind immediately with the message, "Do not worry". I am not a Bible scholar, but I remember reading some Facebook post that stated: "There are 365 verses in the Bible that say, 'Do not worry': one for each day of the year". The verse that I remember the easiest is Jeremiah 29:11 which describes the plan God has for me: the plan to keep me safe from harm and the plans to give me prosperity. That is a rather perfect life, I would say. My thought, "My life is perfect" was not too far from God's plan for my life. I must admit it was comforting to know that the God of the Bible wanted a great future for my life. Yet, another reason I was feeling more and more attracted to His plan.

The deeper you dig into these verses in the Bible that describe the future, you will come to the trump card: Eternal life. If you repeat the thought, "I have eternal life", you will soon begin to experience a sense of euphoria or fearlessness, like you are untouchable. This portrayal is found in the Bible in several places where the description of being at war is mentioned. The acquisition of eternal life requires the acceptance of the power of God and the wisdom of God. These two elements are presented as sacrifice in the person of Jesus Christ: all and all, a very appealing plan.

Two ideas that are pushed forward in the Bible about the future is the kingdom of God and heaven. I am not very clear on the description, but heaven is the place of residence for the Creator where the absence of suffering is absolute, thus giving the idea of pure joy. The idea I receive from reading about the kingdom of God is best described by my untrained mind as the walkway to heaven. Whether the kingdom of God is the walkway to heaven or the kingdom of God is heaven, the reward would end up being the same: the constant presence with the Creator. This is particularly interesting because I have often felt that the repetition of a thought causes the mind to travel in a specific direction dictated by the thought itself. Therefore, if I were to repeat, "I have eternal life and I am bound for heaven", the final destination would be everlasting company with the Creator.

One of the particular conditions for the God-man relationship described in the Bible in multiple verses is the cooperation that must take place. Although the Bible describes God as the Source, the recipient (you or I) must exercise an active role in the process. The Bible repeats, time and time again, that the recipient must ask for and if we have not received the answer, it is because we have not asked for it. This is confirmed in the book of James. This revelation is in particular opposition to what my thinking was before I became aware of the Creative Force and before I started reading the Bible from the idea of the creative process. One of the ideas of God that I grew up with was enforced by my mother, who although a Godly woman was clearly changing what I read in the Bible today. When I found myself in a situation where I had exhausted all my abilities, my mother would reassure that it was in God's will. This meant that God might or might not grant my desire, leaving me vulnerable and begging; please, please, much like a little kid begging from a parent who was unwilling to give. The Bible describes exactly the opposite picture. In multiple verses, the description is that God is willing to give the desires of your heart.

Very often, I hear my patients repeating, "It is in God's hands". This means that they are basically giving up any attempt to change the future as if God was the only one determining the outcome. This is in clear opposition to what I read over and over in the Bible. If I read what the Bible says about my future, it describes that upon entering a relationship with God by the acceptance of Christ, His power and His wisdom, I have the right to call myself a child of God. Clearly, a positive thought. In addition, I am offered the kingdom of God, eternal life, and the warranty that whatever I ask will be given to me. It appears all I have to do is to repeat the request or as the Creative Force teaches, all I have to do is repeat the thought. Thus, my final recommendation about your future would be to repeat the following thought which seems to cover all the fields possible:

"Thank you God, my life is perfect all the time".

CHAPTER TWENTY

PRAYER AND THE CREATIVE FORCE

As you become familiar with the Creative Force, you will begin to experience new situations created by your own ability to repeat a thought. If the thought is positive, the consequences are positive and if the thought is negative, the consequences will be negative. The source of these results has been challenging to distinguish. If we start with the simple thought, "I am making burgers tonight" and you repeat it, your brain will show the steps to take including buying the supplies. The consequence of your actions will be hamburgers. Who was the source? Who put the meat at the store and the buns at the bakery? Since the thinker, most likely, had nothing to do with raising the cow and farming the wheat, the thinker cannot assume absolute credit for the end product. There were separate, creative processes that produced those things, but worked in concert with the thinker who created the final product. Who is this creator or creators? Simple deduction is to assume the presence of other creators in the past who gave us access to the present thinker and made it possible for the present thinker to complete his/her creative process.

If you take the negative thought, "I love to get drunk", the same analysis is possible. Accepting the existence of other creators who did their work of creation, but worked in concert with the present time creator is plausible. Since the outcome would be negative, destructive, it is safe to call this creator or these creators, negative ones. If we begin with the positive thought, "I love my granddaughter", the repetition would result in a motivating energy and some positive actions that would end up in the creation of a safer environment for my granddaughter. That thought became a positive reality. The majority of the materials used to make her environment safe would have been previously created, but since the outcome is positive, the previous Creator or co-creators must have been positive ones.

I learned the idea of the Creator when reading the Bible. In the beginning, the Creator is said to have spoken and his assessment was that the outcome was good. I began to think about the Creator described in the Bible as the positive Creator. However, there are multiple passages in the Bible when the God of the Bible ordered his followers to exterminate other groups of people living in the promised land. If you were a member from those destroyed groups, your conclusion would be that the God of the Bible is a negative creator. In the same manner, if a person begins to repeat the thought, "I need drugs" and the drug dealer appears, the thinker in this circumstance would refer to any previous creators as good creators because their creation has allowed the fulfillment of, "I need drugs". It becomes obvious that we refer to our co-creators as good or bad depending on the thought being repeated by the present thinker.

There are occasions when a thought appears to be incomplete due to the previous creators, whether good or bad, not doing what we expected them to do. The opposite is true on occasions when a situation occurs, not requested, yet encountered in our reality without asking for it. The latter would occur as experienced when a person receives the diagnosis of cancer or a girl gets dumped by her boyfriend. Since the Creative Force teaches that all things are created by thought, it is easy to conclude that our reality may be affected by other co-creators, but that relationship is not clearly understood, yet.

One such example that I personally recall occurred when a nephew received the diagnosis of cancer. I began to pray to the God of the Bible, as did many other members of our family. In spite of the intense repetition of my prayer, the ultimate result was his demise. The question that lingered in my brain was "Why did He not answer my prayer or my repetition?". What became of my creative process? How did other people successfully pray and how did the Creator choose? Many unanswered questions remain and my research into thinking and its power continues. I decided to study the God of the Bible in order to understand better because clearly, the God of my childhood apparently chose to ignore my request. Did I ask wrong? Am I praying to a God of my own making, incapable of answering my request and unable to co-create with me?

Another observation that I have made while teaching thinking in the addiction group is a very similar frustration experienced by most addicts, who hate the addiction, yet are incapable of stopping it. The Creative Force clearly teaches me that the outcome is exactly equal to the thought. If the thought is, "I am fat", the results would be that I get fatter. If the thought is, "I need healing", the outcome is that I am going to feel more sick because the need for healing gets worse.

I chose to study the God of the Bible since my interest in His way of thinking was clearly along the creative process and Creative Force. The thing that I had learned at this point was that the God of the Bible requires a relationship and not the mere knowledge of the existence of God. The God of the Bible also requires an active role in the process. This is clearly expressed multiple times in the Bible: **WITH God all things are possible**. Please note that the Bible does not read: **FOR** God all things are possible. The re-establishment of the connection to the God of the Bible also requires the acceptance of His wisdom and His power, Christ. Once these three conditions are met, the God of the Bible appears to offer a good deal. The King James version of Mark 11:24 begins with, "Whatsoever ye desires". It suggests that the God of the Bible has no limits in what He is willing to offer you.

Matthew 7:7 expresses the three ways necessary to ask in order to receive, very similar to what I found in the book of James. It is stated in James that we do not have because we do not ask. The Bible emphasizes the role I must play, as co-creator, is the requirement for asking. This really begins to narrow the range of answers that I would expect from the God of the Bible. My observations were that The God of the Bible does not answer most people because the majority of them have not made the choice to accept the God of the Bible as the Creator they choose to follow. It was also clear that the God of the Bible does not give everyone equal portions; unlike a socialist God who would offer equal benefits to all.

All of these observations would suggest that if I follow the God of the Bible and I have chosen to accept Christ, and if I ask, would I get whatever I want? A clear limitation appeared in my head. The God of the Bible appears to be the source of only those things contained within the plans He has for me. The God of the Bible clearly cannot be the co-creator if I am asking for something outside the plan He has for me. Furthermore, the God of the Bible is not going to stop you if you are doing something outside His plans for you. Again, it appears that the active role I play in the process is to ask, but the God of the Bible is clearly not going to grant me the things that are harmful to me. In the book of James, it is expressed that God is the source of every perfect and good gift. Since I, the thinker, have the choice to repeat good or bad thoughts, the God of the Bible is the co-creator of only the good things in my life. The bad things in my life are clearly the result of the repetition of my negative thinking in association with a negative, destructive co-creator. One could refer to the negative co-creator as satan or devil, giving me the pivotal job of choosing the thoughts to repeat.

Many Christians frequently pray or repeat thoughts such as, "It is in God hands" giving absolute control to God, the good co-creator, yet the Bible directly expresses the opposite. The human must ask in order for God to co-create with the human thinker. I suspect that many of the requests go unanswered because of this human, hands- off approach. Frequently, we retreat when we do not wish to do what we know we must do. The Creative Force changes the picture because it teaches that one must play an active role in the creative process. Since it is my thinking that has the power to change my reality, I must maintain an active relationship with God.

Following the instructions written in the Bible as how to ask or pray, I decided to test them in order to be able to understand the obvious disconnection between the human thinker and God the good co-creator. Mark 11:24 gave us the central method. The NIV translation reads that I must ask as if I have already received and it promises that whatever I request would be given to me. Personally, I have difficulty understanding some of the poetic ways these verses are written, so I am going to offer my interpretation of Mark 11:24. The Cardenas version of this verse would read, "When you repeat a thought (prayer), repeat it in the past tense as if you have already received and it (the request) will be given to you". I could relate better to my version especially due to the fact that I was testing the Creative Force. I began to ask in the past tense, without limits, and within the plans that God had for me. I clearly knew that if I had chosen to ask for example, to get drunk, The God of the Bible was going to stay out of that process, especially since the Bible clearly reads, "Do not get drunk".

My new prayer became: "Thank you God, I am blessed by everyone, everywhere, all the time. Today, I am wiser, kinder, meeker, stronger, healthier, wealthier and fearless. Thank you father that my children are pillars of society. Thank you father that I am blessed by my wife all the time in every way." The rest is history. My part was repetition using my own voice. I am happy to report that after a few weeks of repetition things began to appear differently. My confidence went up, my relationship with my wife continues to grow, and my children are walking the straight and narrow path to success. I am blessed with a beautiful, gracious granddaughter. I have to admit that initially I was scared when all the things I had requested were coming my way. Quickly, I came to the realization that the promises of the God of the Bible are true. Today, I continue to repeat my prayer with the confidence that the God of the Bible, my good co-creator, seems to be very near me. It is as if He is almost by my side, as my protector, guide, source, teacher, precreating the things I need in order for me to co-create the good things for which I chose to ask within his plans for me.

My ability to trust the God of the Bible continues to grow and His grace is poured into my life again and again making it true that I am blessed by everyone, everywhere, all the time. I no longer fear the future. My future is created by my God in addition to my thinking. My elimination of negative thoughts and their replacement with only positive thoughts makes my future brighter and brighter. I now live in a reality that allows me to scream, "Thank you God my life is better and better" much like the plan He prescribed for my life.

CHAPTER TWENTY ONE

REARING CHILDREN AND THE CREATIVE FORCE

After recognizing the creative process, I quickly began to experience the rewards of using the Creative Force correctly. My immediate desire was to teach this finding to anyone who would listen to me. My children fell victim to my motivation and I began to experiment with them, on them, for them. The first question that came to my mind was, "Can I change other people?". Remember, that questions are points of origin for thoughts and depending on your answer, your brain will travel in the specific direction to put those thoughts into action. What your brain will see is the steps you are required to take to make the thought become your reality. At this point, I had the answer to the question I had been pondering. "I cannot change people" was the old thought that needed to be dropped. I said to myself, "What do I have to lose?". So, I settled on "Yes, I can change people".

The result of this repetition was that I felt a motivation to become engaged with suffering people. I had become aware that my thoughts did not change the actions of others, but my actions caused by my thoughts did have the power to change the thinking of others. As the result of my awareness that the power was in the repetition of thoughts and with the close contact I had with my children, they were my first students. The work done with my children was the basis for writing the first chapter, The Work That Must Be Done. Without going into too much detail, changes nothing short of miracles, began to occur. I am happy to repeat that my children are probably my best work, yet we continue to move toward success without limits. The repetition of positive thoughts, eternal thoughts should never end.

After starting to see success, I felt a sense of anger that I had wasted my previous energy and time before learning about the Creative Force. My mind wondered, why someone, anyone did not or would not tell me about such force? The creative process seems to be so logical. I felt cheated that no one seemed to be aware of this force. Every time, I taught someone about this force, their answer would be one of surprise and wonder. It is so simple, yet so important, so powerful. This made me realize that I was becoming that someone I had wished for earlier in my life when my children were younger. I felt the motivation and purpose to continue speaking about this force created by thought repetition.

One of the initial steps in my development was to question the thoughts with which I had grown up. I remember repeating, "I cannot change people" and "Children come without instructions". If you repeat, "Children come without instructions", now, you can predict what will happen. My reality became a state of confusion. Like most parents, I hoped that my children would travel the straight and narrow path. At that time, I was personally looking for that road myself. In my heart I felt anxiety, but I would calm my heart by saying to myself that at the very least I was giving them a good example. I gave myself peace by repeating the thought, "I am doing my best". Little did I know that particular thought was very bad in itself.

If you repeat, "I am doing my best", or any other repeated thought, your brain will show you what to do. This particular thought reveals to you that nothing new should be done. Therefore, you keep on doing the very same things you have been doing in the past. You do not see the need to change direction or position. The end result is that you continue to get exactly the same results that you have been getting all along. It is like a vicious cycle. It is very frustrating when you see your children deviating from what you wished, yet unable to see what the right action is. Doubt and fear become your partners in parenting.

I remember that I began to experiment with two thoughts, "I am a better and better parent" and "My children are pillars of society". The results began to happen quickly. I began to feel the responsibility to train my children and I felt the confidence of my authority. It was almost like hearing other parents repeating to themselves when a little one is having a tantrum, "I am the adult". I quickly went from friend to teacher. Every action and spoken word had intention and purpose. Initially, there was some friction, but as my children reported later, it developed a sense of trust in them. That was when I began to notice that my actions were affecting their thinking.

Later on, as I began to study thoughts, the size of the thoughts; the power of repetition; and the creation of an environment that led to that repetition, I became convinced that not only did I have the responsibility of training my children, but I also had the ability. I felt capable. I now knew what to teach and how to teach. Prior to learning the power of the Creative Force, my focus had been on my career, money, and success. Now, that I was aware of the Creative Force, my focus had become focused on their thinking and particularly the thoughts they were repeating. I went from worrying about the things of this world (things that every human worries about) to worrying about the things that make up our character. It was almost like I had developed a laser eye, capable of penetrating directly to the core of the problem. I found it amusing that I was less concerned with results or actions as much as I was concerned with thoughts. It was easy to forgive an action and I became absolutely focused on pointing out the thoughts that caused that action, thus requiring the change of thought.

I remember having to change their thinking from, "I cannot" to "I can do all things". I had to require honesty, no stealing, helping the poor, loving your neighbors, forgiving all the time, demanding work and encouraging them to dream without limits. I found myself attracted to the things that the Bible was teaching only to find myself affirmed by my actions. Today, I have not doubt in my heart that my children know there is energy in thinking, I have no doubt of what the future will bring them. I have the confidence that they will become teachers of men because they have felt the power of creation. As they begin to try to influence people, they are going to find their purpose and direction easily.

A pattern was developing in my experimentation with the creative process. As I began experimenting with any thought and I became aware of the results, I would quickly find affirmation in the Bible. It was not different when it came to training my children. I began to notice for example, the thought, "I can do all things because I have the power of God and the wisdom of God" was contrary to the thoughts they have been repeating. The expressions, "I cannot" or "I am afraid" were frequently heard in my house prior to learning about the Creative Force. "Love one another" was in contradiction to their thinking, "I hate such and such". The examples of such changes are plentiful, but the final conclusion was that the thoughts of the Bible were the positive thoughts for which I was looking. It was rather amazing to find all the thoughts I was looking for in one place, so neatly put together. You have no choice but to be amazed that all of these thoughts were placed in one place, in such a neat sequence, over a period of thousands of years. Who would do that? The answer from the Creative Force is obvious: a creator, the good, all powerful, all knowing, good creator; my Creator.

The book of Joshua chapter one, verse eight puts it all together. It reads, "This book of instructions (**thought**) must not depart from your mouth. You are to recite it day and night (**repeat**), that you might be able to do (**action**) everything written in it, for then you will prosper and succeed (**outcome**)". A similar explanation is given in Psalm one with more poetry. I was beginning to recognize that these instructions had been there for a long time and that the problem with my thinking was not the lack of training, but rather my lack of wisdom. I was unable to understand the things that many had attempted to teach me over the years. I have to warn you that as I began to read the Bible things got worse. It was not that I was not experiencing success, but rather that it became more obvious that the things that are needed to teach my children had been in the Bible for centuries, but somehow I had missed them. I learned in Psalm 78:5-6 that God exhorts us to teach these commandments to our children, even those yet to be born, so that the next generation would know them and in turn, teach them to their children.

I was thinking of my own learning process from childhood to present time. I assume it began with my mother teaching me to pray; then the nuns giving Bible lessons; next to the dinners at the First Baptist Church in Bowling Green that I was invited to as an international student; and finally, to the Bible study teachers in my adult life. The time passed spanned over 40 years and the number of times that I had heard the message would be probably in the hundreds. All of that energy and all of that effort culminated in creating who I am today. At this point, it was very clear in my mind that I had not heard the message because I did not want to hear the message. It was not the lack of the message or the weakness of the messenger. There seems to have been plenty of both. Finally, all their efforts came to fruition. I declare myself a believer of the God of the Bible. He is an awesome Creator responsible for putting such a neat and perfect group of thoughts all in one place so that we, present day creators, do not have to wander far to find all the instructions needed to lead a successful life. This is what I had to teach my children and what All of us should be teaching all the children of this world.

The God of the Bible gives me a plan for my life: Go make disciples. If I take myself as an example, it took many years, many attempts, by many people to connect me to the right Creator. As a result, I have developed an attitude of relationship to all of those who have tried, are trying, and will continue to try to figure out life without the compass that the great Creator provides. The Creator described in the Bible appears to have given me a second chance, third chance, fourth chance, and on and on. This Creator never gave up on me. That is the attitude one must take when making disciples, especially our children. My final exhortation is to teach your children to repeat only the thoughts given to us by the great Creator, the great I AM.

CHAPTER TWENTY TWO

RACISM

One of my early goals in life, as a child, was to be a part of the solution ending poverty. This was at a time when I would think that all things are possible. This idea had never left my brain, but it moved up and down in my priority list depending on what else was on my plate. Upon learning about the Creative Force and the creative process, I began to experiment with these processes, especially during my practice of medicine. When I was giving any type of counseling, I could not help but focus on the number of negative thoughts spoken by my patients. My brain, like a trained ninja, would automatically begin to respond with my inside voice, the ill effects yet to come if the negative thinking was to continue. After much observation, I began to see a pattern. Those who suffer the most, complain the most. It became a case of the chicken and the egg; which was first? The creative process makes the answer obvious: the complaining was first, followed by the repetitions, followed by negative actions, and finally, the negative consequences were the outcome.

As a trained scientist, I decided to extend my observation for many more years until I was able to determine: if the observation remained consistent as to make it a general rule that those who complained the most also suffered the most. It was during this time of observation that I began to pay attention to the civic leaders of the time, especially those who were speaking about race. I began to observe the consistency of the complaining. The news provided coverage to some of these figures, with an intense effort to make them known to everyone. In contrast, my analysis was rather simple because I was only using the Creative Force to determine my sympathy or apathy for their cause.

It is well known that prior to 1970, there were laws that discriminated against citizens of the USA based on the color of their skin, but the same cannot be said for the present time. If anyone knows about such laws, please let me know. I do not claim knowledge of every law. Therefore, the question that lingers in my mind is, "Why after 50 years are there some people still complaining?". From the sociological point of view, two generations have passed, but in someone's mind, time was sitting still and the problems continue to affect today's youth and some others. To those people, the problem seems worse than it was 50 plus years ago. All of this happened around me when I was going to college with many "so called" minorities. It was confusing to me when I heard the complaints by some minority leaders while at the same time, many including myself, were enjoying no obstacles due to our race.

I could not help but to think of one of the heroes in my life, my father. He left his home by age 12 moving away from an environment affected by alcohol and anger while some of his siblings with less sense of adventure stayed behind. Moving time forward some 60 years, I find that my father was enjoying an incredible amount of success in most parts of his life while his siblings had, at best, continued the same pathway as their parents. It was not until some 15 years ago, when I became aware of the Creative Force that I found the explanation for the different outcomes of my father and his siblings. I clearly remember my father constantly repeating, almost to himself, what appears to be his mantra, "We are doing fine". Presently, my father, at age 83 continues to work daily even putting some of my siblings to shame in spite of the age difference.

The conclusion that was becoming rather obvious to me was that there are only two types of individuals in the world and race has nothing to do with this. There are positive thinkers and there are negative thinkers.

The mechanics of the problem of racism or what people call racism in the USA is easy to describe. If you take an angry, unemployed, unmotivated young person of any race and you place that person as the outcome of the Creative Force, one would quickly understand that his/her outcome was only possible due to his/her actions. His/her action was the result of the thoughts that he/she was repeating. In the same way, I can predict the thought he/she was repeating considering I know that the thought and the outcome are equal. In general terms, this disenfranchised individual must be repeating the thought, "I am a victim of the system". The system was seen as everything outside his/her control: the government, the police, the schools, and basically any successful individual, rich or poor, who is not sharing the same thoughts as the system. This specific thought, "the system" also is impenetrable, indestructible, and impossible to beat in the minds of the young thinker. Many people never change this thought and live with it their whole life. Since it is a negative thought, the actions it produces are negative and the outcomes are negative. To the poor thinker, it makes no difference that some of his/her peers that came up through the same system are capable of achieving success. It is simply the fault of the system. The only excuse I would give to these negative thinkers is that up until today, thinking is not taught in school. I am confident that, with this book and many others to follow, we will begin to focus on the real problem: poor thinking.

If any individual; regardless of race, regardless of gender, regardless of religion, regardless of nation of origin who repeats this thought over time, his/her brain is only going to show him/her the choices that fulfill the thought. Please note that this is predicted by the CARDENAS LAW. The brain not only shows limited opportunities, but the brain would also give the motivation to select the choices that would make him/her victims in their own mind. The solution is rather simple, yet it is hidden from most leaders because they do not seem to be aware of the Creative Force. The simple solution is for the "so called victim" to change his/her thinking.

Instead of creating methods of changing how we think, other solutions were promoted by the government. Over the last 50 years and after much discussion, those officials put in place programs creating opportunities intended to change the reality rather than the thinking. Unaware that those individuals were not able to take advantage of the opportunities because they had been repeating the thought, "I am a victim of the system". Most politicians, with their best intentions and their best thinking, continue to invest in such programs while repeating that poor people are victims of the system. Is this harmful? In the previous chapters, I had taught you that my thinking has no power over your thinking and that fact remains true. My actions, however, do affect your thinking. When a leader continually speaks of the youth being victims, the youth, that has already been thinking, "I am a victim of the system", continues to repeat and enforce that thought making the creative energy stronger and creating victims of many races. Yes, I fault the leaders who spew hate and negativity about the system which they, themselves created over the last 50 years.

One complicating factor in this process is the role of the mass media and even more intense is the role of the social media. As the number of repetitions goes up, so does the creative energy. Due to the fact that the original thought is negative, the energy generated by the intense repetition is negative. The actions generated are negative and so are the results. Black youth, Hispanic youth, or White youth who feel disenfranchised default to violence as a result of their negative thinking. Finally, the violence has no race; thinking has no race; and the suffering has no race. Thus suffering continues because those young people do not seem to be aware of the Creative Force.

What is very interesting to me is that I went to school with young black men and women, young Hispanic men and women who rose above the general odds of their success. Why were those young people born in the same country, coming from the same neighborhoods able to rise above the others of similar race and background? The same question could be asked in my father's situation? How did that 12 year old runaway end up so successful? The answers become easy to see, if you are aware of the creative process and the Creative Force. However, the answer is hidden if you do not know: it is all determined by your thinking.

Is the solution easy and known? Of course it is; the best recent example was given to me by Mr. Morgan Freeman in an interview he did with Harry Reasoner. Mr. Freeman said: "Stop calling me a black man and I will stop calling you a white man".

In others words, racial thoughts should disappear. Do not even mention it. If you do not repeat the thought, the energy generated by previous repetitions will disappear. Imagine what would happen if the mass media and the social media were to stop using race to cause division. It is easy to imagine. We all would stop seeing race as the cause of the problem. Would this cause the problems of hate to go away? Not at all; especially if people continued to repeat that they were victims of the system. Race would just stop being a factor in excuses. Personal characteristics would be used to create the explanation why you are or you are not as successful as the person sitting next to you. Unless everyone is familiar with the Creative Force and the creative process, we all will wonder and blame others for our lack of success.

Why are the young people that I went to college with different from the young people who are less successful? Why was my father more successful than his siblings in spite of the odds. The answer comes from the creative process: the difference lies in different thinking. I began to focus on the successful people's thinking and the pattern of success began to flow quickly. One common factor that yelled, "Look at me" was the fact that the successful youth were all church going. When I thought about my father, he really was not a church attender per say, but he has always been a man with a very deep faith in the power of the Virgin Mary, the mother of Christ. The common thread appears to be the knowledge and expectation of favor by a power greater than oneself.

How do we acquire that connection? For most people of faith, our trip begins at home. This was true for the young people I went to school with. In general, it is a set of good parents who connect you to God as a child, but it does not have to be your blood parents. Any parental figure who transfers their way of thinking to the next generation is capable of that influence. I often repeat in my lectures that since my parents chose to keep me as a child in spite of my bad behaviors, their influence molded me. They did not quit training me until I was a mature adult. I must accept that I was given more than most. Therefore, my success is the gift given to me by my Creator who saw fit to give me two exemplary parents as a child. My mother taught me about God and my father taught me that I was capable of achieving my dreams. They drilled in me the existence of God, the Creator and also my ability to achieve by hard work.

Going back to the young people who claim to be victims of the system and regardless of their race, the question to answer is, can I change them? Is there anything that can be done? The Creative Force gives you the answer. It is a big yes. The initial step is to cause them to change their thinking. The next step is to create an environment where the more positive thinking is repeated. It would be like re-parenting in the manner that most of us successful individuals were parented. The best description that comes to mind for this process would be more like making disciples.

Making disciples seems to be a process that begins with earning someone's trust. It also requires the presentation of new thinking and ends with the repetition of the new thinking. What thoughts should I teach when making disciples? What are the thoughts that made me successful? Again, the Creative Force teaches you that positive thinking gives you positive results. It also teaches that larger thoughts create bigger results. The one thought that comes to mind immediately is, "I can do all things because I have the power of God and the wisdom of God". This particular thought removes all possible excuses I could create with my thinking. It does not hurt if I repeat that, "The plans God has for me are to keep me safe and to make me prosperous". In conclusion, I return full circle to the dependency and trust in the thinking that is taught in the Bible. Therefore, the church has the power, the ability, and the mission to fix this particular problem of the human condition not only here in the USA, but also anywhere in the world where we find people suffering from poor thinking.

CHAPTER TWENTY THREE

THOUGHTS TO AVOID AND THOUGHTS TO REPEAT

When I became aware of the Creative Force, I began to notice that many people at different times were able to see glimpses of the creative process. I heard the power of positive thinking, yet no one had warned me about the power of its counterpart, the negative thinking. Zig Ziglar comes to mind as one of the recent examples. The motivational speeches I gave when I coached my daughter's soccer team contained bits of the process yet at that time, I did not possess the whole method. I remember coming across similar descriptions especially in the business world. You start with a vision, create a mission statement, draw your plan of action, and then you evaluate the outcome. Unfortunately, the writers of these business methods were not aware of the big picture. What is the big picture? The big picture is that your reality has been created by all of your thinking; No exceptions.

In reading the book, *The Master Key System*, I was attracted to a particular statement that was expressed almost as in passing. The author of this book wrote that power comes from knowing that you have the power. Let it sink in for a couple of minutes. The explanation is that the first step in this process is to accept that thoughts have energy. If you do not accept it, you will continue to think without the awareness that you are the author of your reality. Not being aware that you are the author of your reality does not remove the consequences of your thinking. Once you become aware of this power, your power, you will begin the process of analyzing basically every thought that comes out of your mouth. You should run those thoughts through the mirror exercise. You will quickly become aware that a negative thought does not have to be mean or derogatory. I remember when I was obese I repeated, "I love brownies". The result was that there was no safe brownie within ten miles of my presence and even if full, I would eat it making my obesity worse. As soon as I became aware of the power of thinking, I changed the thought to, "I hate brownies". I know I am using the word hate, but the consequence of that particular thought was that I no longer was attracted to the brownie or a victim of it. I found freedom from that food addiction and I became healthier. In order to determine if a particular thought is good or bad, we must begin by looking at the thinker and predict the reality created by the thought. It is the combination of the thinker plus the thought that determines if we should continue to repeat a particular thought depending on the overall goals spoken by the thinker/creator.

In general terms, the thoughts to be avoided are those which: cause dependency, limitations, weakness, and obstacles; thoughts of hate; thoughts of unrestrained pleasure; thoughts that would break the law if they were to become reality; thoughts that cause separation among family members; thoughts of unforgiveness; selfish thoughts; thoughts of destruction instead of creation; irresponsible thoughts; thoughts that cause fear, distrust, or separation; thoughts of sickness; ungrateful thoughts; thoughts of finality and fatality; thoughts of hopelessness; thoughts of loneliness; thoughts of impatience; thoughts that cause shame, guilt, or anger; thoughts that create envy; proud thoughts; dishonest thoughts and lies; and any thoughts with tiny fields of action. I think that if I were to take the time, I could write negative thoughts from here to eternity and I would never finish the list. Instead, my goal is to train you to create the opposite, only positive thoughts and to train you to become aware of the difference.

There are a few examples to discuss at this point to train you in the creation of positive thoughts:

"Thank you God my life is perfect all the time". This particular thought begins with the words "my life." The field of action is complete and leaves nothing out to chance. The word, "perfect" emphasizes a level of excellence that could hardly be improved except semantically, but not practically. I have said, "My life is perfecter", but the degree of perfection really is difficult to visualize. This thought ends with, "all the time". Those particular words allows this thought to acquire a huge field of action. "My life" makes this thought an eternal thought, without end. All and all a very positive thought highly recommended for repetition. The field of action can be made smaller by changing the subject. For example: I can say, "Thank you God I look perfect all the time" and the field of action would be limited to my physical looks. I hope you get the point.

Another thought that I want you to consider is: "Thank you God

my life is better and better". Again, the field of action is self explanatory, but "better and better" denotes an always ascending path to a higher degree of better. For example, in terms of money, if today I have $100,000, tomorrow I would be expecting better or $100,001. Again, the field of action can be limited simply by changing the subject, or the time concept. As another example:
"My wife is better and better"
"My truck is better and better"
"My job is better and better"
"My health is better and better"
"My children are doing better and better".

Better and better gives the idea of always improving without the complaint that things are bad. Complaining of any kind would be considered negative thinking. My favorite thought or expression that I know is grammatically incorrect is, "Thank you God I am blesseder and blesseder all the time". Sometimes, I write it as, "Thank you God I am blesseder times blesseder all the time". I really have little concern for those who think it is grammatically incorrect because their thinking has no effect on my thinking. Since I like that expression, it gets repeated frequently and therefore, it produces the consequence that I feel blesseder all the time.

In my search for more and more positive thoughts, thoughts with big fields of action and eternal thoughts, I was led to the Bible. I found a ton of them. It is really difficult to choose between so many. One that got my attention was 1 Corinthians, 2:16. It states, "I have the mind of Christ". Let that thought simmer for a bit. If I have the mind of Christ easily acquired by repetition, clearly my thinking would move in a direction different from its natural course when used to repeat only my thoughts. Again, I am intentionally limiting re-writing verses from the Bible because the reader has access to it easily. By now, I was beginning to see a pattern that most of what I thought to be positive was easily found in the Bible causing me to become even more attracted to it than I was before. My conclusion is that if you wonder if a thought is positive, confirm its positivity by comparing it to the truths found in the Bible. If you can refute it by something found in the Bible, my recommendation is to stop considering it worthy of repetition. In the final analysis, if you find yourself unable to come to a direct answer, I would suggest to repeat it and observe any behavioral changes it causes to find the reality it creates. If you find that the reality it created to be negative or harmful, go back to the drawing board and start by changing the thought. Now you are the master of your own creation.

THANK YOU FATHER, TODAY I AM WISER AND WISER.

CHAPTER TWENTY FOUR

CONCLUSION

Fifteen years ago, my life, just as the lives of most people, included the good, the bad, and the ugly. I was enjoying success in some areas and absolute failure in others. In my attempts to fix the broken parts of my life, my search led to reading book after book, always questioning, always wondering and always failing. The failures felt more intense than the satisfaction felt in the areas of success. My search for genuine satisfaction led to the Bible and to church, only to give partial improvement in some areas while making others more confusing. I lived with fear and anxiety. I ate my pain away, not much different than those people who use alcohol, drugs, or any other addiction for that matter. Inside, I felt hopeless while the outside kept the smile on trying to find lasting satisfaction while chasing the things that this world has to offer. I chased wealth, power, and pleasure. The satisfaction was temporary. I had accepted Christ, yet I did not feel much change and the temptations of this world kept on winning the fight.

Fifteen years ago I became aware of the energy contained in some thoughts and I began to see the creative process. I began to experiment with thought and I felt its power. It began with my ability to control my body shape, my weight, my diet, and my exercise. My excitement led me to teach a weight loss program. I continued the experimentation and I continued to grow. More and more areas of my life were coming under control. The observation that the energy generated affected only the thinker, moved me dramatically forward. Finding the size of thoughts gave further understanding. I began to repeat, "I am wiser and wiser". I was led to find that the creative process I had formulated was written in black and white in the Bible.

I began to use the creative process to help addicted people find their way out of addiction. In addition, I began to apply this process to train my children. There were plenty of nights that I fell asleep repeating, "I am a better and better father and my children are pillars of society". The relationship with my children, the quality of their lives, and the strength of their purpose grew quickly. I began to see success in more areas. One critical point in my walk was when I found in the book of Romans that Christ is the power of God and the wisdom of God. I felt the inclination to re-write the verse that was confusing to me up to that point. I re-wrote Philippians 4:13 as, "I can do all things because I have the power of God and the wisdom of God". Finally, I understood the gift of God. Finally, I became aware that all my problems had been created by my thinking. The confirmation of that fact came not only from the Creative Force, but also directly from Jesus Christ in Matthew 15:19.

I began a process of cleaning my thinking by the renewing of my mind as it is suggested in Romans 12:2. The change basically included every thought. In 2 Corinthians 10:5. It teaches that every thought must be analyzed and changed if it is different from what is taught by Christ. The process became clear and my life became clear. The fears that I once felt became smaller and smaller. My confidence in my success went through the roof, but my definition of success changed. I had found my purpose in life. The things I used to chase such as power, pleasure, and possessions grew dimmer and dimmer. I began to search for the things of the kingdom of God: love, wisdom, and faith. Now, I have received the proper instructions for a successful trip here on Earth while moving heaven bound where I will come face to face with my Creator. In the mean time, I will exercise my purpose and I will continue to make disciples.

Now you know.

Kindly,

Dr. C.

Are you tired of your struggles with life?

YOU ARE NOT ALONE.

Your answer has been in your head all along.

Colombian by birth, American by choice, Christian by grace. Jorge Cardenas, M.D., FACOG received his bachelor's degree from Western Kentucky University, attended DREW/UCLA to receive his medical education, and then completed his residency training and board certification. Fellow of the American College of Ob/Gyn since 1990, he has been engaged in private practice in Paducah, Kentucky for the past 22 years.

www.ingramcontent.com/pod-product-compliance
Lightning Source LLC
Chambersburg PA
CBHW071358160426
42811CB00111B/2214/J